SURVIVORS

The forgotten victims of murder & suspicious deaths

Shocking true stories about America's
pursuit of police transparency & justice

DENNIS N. GRIFFIN
with
THE TRANSPARENCY PROJECT

FOREWORD BY
LYNDA CHELDELIN FELL
INTERNATIONAL GRIEF INSTITUTE

SURVIVORS

The forgotten victims of murder & suspicious deaths – 1st ed.
Dennis N. Griffin with The Transparency Project
www.AlyBlueMedia.com

Cover Design by AlyBlue Media, LLC
Interior Design by AlyBlue Media LLC
Published by AlyBlue Media, LLC

ISBN: 978-1-950712-01-4
AlyBlue Media, LLC
Ferndale, WA 98248
www.AlyBlueMedia.com

PRINTED IN THE UNITED STATES OF AMERICA

Testimonials

"STARTING POINT . . . The survivors of victims of murder and suspicious death are often victimized twice: first by the loss of their loved one and subsequently by the system they rely on for justice. The stories told in *Survivors* serve to expose the shortcomings in our justice system that seem to provide the suspects and perpetrators of crimes with all the protections, while the survivors don't have a voice and are left to their own devices. It is time for that to change and the playing field to be leveled. This book is a good starting point." —LARRY YOUNG, Justice For Molly & advocate for Molly's Law

"MEANINGFUL . . . *Survivors* goes beyond the storytelling of cases and speaks to the appalling experiences surviving victims have faced within our criminal justice system. The work of The Transparency Project is empowering the surviving families and uniting them to bring forth meaningful changes that will be in effect for the future." —DELILAH JONES, Producer and Co-host of The Transparency Project and Crime Wire radio podcasts

"NECESSARY . . . Many unsolved murders are solved when someone picks up the telephone and calls in a tip. *Survivors* will generate the necessary publicity for someone to come forward with information that will identify the person(s) responsible for these unsolved homicides." —GENE CERVANTES, advocate with Citizens Against Homicide

"UNWAVERING . . . *Survivors* is a collection of first-hand experiences detailing the unthinkable horrors shared by those who have lost a loved one to murder or suspicious death, and the unwavering determination required to navigate a flawed justice system in their quest for answers, a sense of closure, and peace." —KELLY O'KEEFE, producer at Kelly Vision Productions

"IMPORTANT . . . The Transparency Project is doing important work in bringing this issue to the attention of the public. Thank you for your efforts." —ROMAN MARTIN, author of *UNDERWORLD—How to Survive and Thrive in the American Mafia*

"VITAL . . . Generating public awareness with books like *Survivors* not only gives the family a voice, it can provide leads to law enforcement. Some cases can go cold for decades without that one vital clue." —SYNOVA CANTRELL, true crime author and advocate

"CATALYST FOR CHANGE . . . *Survivors* details the unfathomable tragedies experienced by families and survivors of loved ones who have been a victim of murder, and are looking for answers and justice from a judicial system in crisis. The book is a catalyst for change as it brings systemic issues to the forefront with strategies of how constituencies can work together to ultimately bring victimized families hope for resolution," —KAREN STORSTEEN, M.S., M.A., Psychotherapist and Intuitive Management Consultant

SURVIVORS

Dedication

This book is dedicated to the victims of murder and suspicious deaths whose cases have gone inactive or cold, and to their survivors who continue to struggle in pursuit of resolution and justice for their lost loved ones. May God bless them and keep them strong.

Contents

Foreword

"9-1-1. What's your emergency?"

"My neighbor isn't breathing. I think he killed himself. There's an electrical cord around his neck."

When responding to calls like the one above, one can't help but arrive with a psychological assumption that the cause of death was self-inflicted or perhaps accidental. The sequence of events then proceed based on one or the other. After all, it's human nature to rush judgment and assumptions. But when there's more than meets the eye, the danger of preconceived notions is that they leave us vulnerable to critical errors in thinking. Finding the truth relies on a thorough and meticulous evidence-based search through facts that allow no room for assumption.

Arguably, keeping an open mind is one of the most powerful—and difficult things—to practice in any profession. In law enforcement, however, such tendencies can result in incomplete investigations that leave society vulnerable. The real criminal remains at large, and traumatized families crying foul face a secondary injustice caused by those paid to protect them.

When evidence doesn't prove cause of death beyond shadow of a doubt, why do detectives choose to trivialize family pleas? Sometimes it's simply due to lack of resources or manpower. Sometimes when an investigation is botched, internal affairs wants to conceal it from hungry media. Sometimes it's due to police corruption or perhaps a C.S.I. effect in which the criminal used televised techniques to stage the scene, remove trace evidence, and outsmart investigators.

No matter the reason, too many deaths are wrongfully concluded with case closed.

The stories in this book expose the truth behind the alarming number of unsolved murders and suspicious deaths erroneously classified as natural, accidental, or self-inflicted with little to no investigation. It's a shocking read, but necessary.

Change begins with raising awareness and using voices to amplify a problem, no matter how good, bad, or ugly. That's the intent behind sharing these stories—to raise awareness about a growing problem.

The duty to do something has been courageously put into motion by Dennis Griffin. Now retired after twenty years in law enforcement, he refuses to remain silent any longer. In his quest to help families find answers, he reveals the secrecies that exist in law enforcement on his show Crime Wire. And now he's doing it between the covers of this book. In the name of justice and to help those whose cries have gone ignored, Dennis Griffin is an agent of change.

May families who have been trivialized find comfort in knowing their voices are no longer silent.

LYNDA CHELDELIN FELL
International Grief Institute
www.LyndaFell.com

Introduction

The primary goal of this book is not to solve the specific cold cases you will read about. These stories do, however, serve to illustrate and bring attention to problems within the justice system that need to be addressed. It is my hope that through public awareness and legislation (such as Molly's Law), the playing field can be leveled and give these contributors and all the other forgotten victims out there (and future survivors), a better opportunity to obtain true justice. This will be a monumental task, make no mistake. However, it has to begin somewhere. Let it be here.

If you do find yourself in a similar situation, there are a few things you can do to give yourself the best chance for resolution:

- Don't be overbearing, but keep in contact with the investigator(s) handling your case.

- Keep detailed notes, copies of emails, etc., of your contact with law enforcement officials.

- If you are having issues in dealing with the police, contact a victim advocacy organization to intervene on your behalf. There are several highly dedicated nonprofit groups who can help you.

- Research the laws in your state. Find out the statute of limitations to file a civil wrongful death lawsuit and learn what records you are entitled to see and how to obtain them.

- Don't let frustration or intimidation cause you to throw in the towel. Keep on top of things and don't give up.

I first became involved with cold case investigations in 2010, when I was asked by my boss at Forensic Consulting Specialties in Syracuse, New York, to look into the March 2007 death of U.S. Army Sergeant Patrick Rust.

Assigned to the 10th Mountain Division headquartered at Fort Drum in Watertown, New York, Patrick had recently returned home from deployment in Afghanistan when he went missing. His skeletal remains were found six months later. His cause and manner of death remain undetermined.

My investigation has developed information and questions that need to be addressed by law enforcement. Unfortunately, as of now the authorities have shown little interest in pursuing new leads.

As a result of my experience over the past nine years, my eyes have been opened to the alarming number of currently unsolved murders and suspicious deaths that are not classified as homicides. Equally alarming are the number of deaths that were declared suicides with little or no investigation.

Beginning with my show Crime Wire on Blog Talk Radio and continuing with The Transparency Project Radio programming on the Inside Lenz Network, I profiled many of these cases, giving the families of the victims an opportunity to tell their stories. In dealing with these survivors it became increasing clear to me that many of them have been victimized twice. First by the loss of their loved one, and then by the very system they relied on for resolution. That realization served as the impetus for this book. You will note that nearly all the stories are critical of the investigations done by the authorities; and none have endings—the struggles of the writers for resolution are ongoing.

With only a couple of exceptions, the survivors who contributed stories had no or very limited prior writing experience. I did basic editing in regard to organization, spelling, punctuation, and grammar. Other than that, their accounts are in their own voices and words. You should also be aware that some of the names that appear are aliases, used to protect individual privacy.

Royalties resulting from the sale of this book, after production costs, will be donated to nonprofit victim advocacy organizations.

DENNIS N. GRIFFIN
The Transparency Project
griff1945@hotmail.com

To use the FBI's terminology, the national clearance rate for homicide today is 64.1 percent. Fifty years ago, it was more than 90 percent.

-NPR.org

Molly's Law

On July 19, 2016, then Illinois governor Bruce Rauner signed legislation known as Molly's Law. An Illinois Bar Journal article by Matthew Hector explained the new law this way:

Molly's Law gives some wrongful death claimants more time to sue

Molly's Law gives plaintiffs more time to bring wrongful death cases that stem from some allegedly intentional and criminal conduct and allows disappointed FOIA requesters to ask the attorney general's office to review denials.

March 24, 2012 was a tragic day for the family of Molly Young, a Carbondale woman who died of a gunshot wound to the head. She was found in the apartment of her boyfriend, Richie Minton. The exact circumstances of her death were never determined.

Molly's father, Larry Young, tried to obtain information related to his daughter's death, but his Freedom of Information Act (FOIA) requests took a long time to process. By the time he filed a wrongful death lawsuit against Minton, whom Young believes shot his daughter, the two-year statute of limitations had expired. Young's case was dismissed as untimely.

As a result of his experiences trying to obtain information about the investigation into his daughter's death, Young began advocating for legislation changing how FOIA requests are processed and extending the statute of limitations to bring wrongful death actions. The bills, which were introduced in February, unanimously passed the House in April. Governor Rauner signed the bills into law on July 19, 2016.

TWO NEW PUBLIC ACTS

Public Act 99-0587 is commonly known as "Molly's Law." It amends the Wrongful Death Act, extending the statute of limitations for filing a wrongful death action in certain situations. When an individual dies as the result of violent, intentional conduct, the statute of limitations is extended to five years, as opposed to the normal two-year limitations period. If a criminal case is pending, the limitations period extends to one year after the final disposition of the criminal case. Murder, second degree murder, intentional homicide of an unborn child, both intentional and negligent manslaughter of an unborn child, involuntary manslaughter, and drug-induced homicide qualify for the law's expanded limitations period.

In many cases, it may be difficult or impossible to get information about a case while an investigation is pending. Since the limitations clock starts ticking from the date of the individual's death, long delays can lead to families and other survivors left without an appropriate civil remedy.

However, the statute only extends the limitations period as to the individual who allegedly committed the violent act or was a defendant in a criminal matter. Other parties suspected of having been involved with the allegedly wrongful death are still subject to the two-year limitations period. With multiple possible tortfeasors, parties may need to file separate wrongful death actions to preserve their claims.

Developing claims and obtaining information should be made easier by Molly's Law's companion legislation, Public Act 99-0586, which amends the Freedom of Information Act. Section 9.5 of the Act allows individuals whose FOIA requests are denied to seek review from the attorney general's office. If the AG's office determines that a violation of the Act has occurred, it will issue a binding opinion letter. Under the new amendments, requesters may now file their own actions to enforce those opinion letters. (5 ILCS 140/11(a-5).)

Once an opinion is issued, requesters who file an enforcement action enjoy the rebuttable presumption that the public body willfully and intentionally failed to comply with the Act. (5 ILCS 104/11.6.) The public body may rebut the presumption by showing that it was making a good faith effort to comply, but that it was not possible to do so within 35 days.

Public bodies that fail to rebut that presumption, or those that are found by a court to have willfully and intentionally failed to comply, may be penalized between $2,500 and $5,000 per occurrence. The amendments allow courts to impose additional penalties of up to $1,000 per day for each day the violation continues.

Although the law is not a cure-all, it is a good start by providing the survivors of victims of murder and suspicious deaths with additional tools in their fight for justice.

Because most homicides are state crimes, efforts to get laws such as this enacted require a state-by-state effort. If you would like more information about Molly's Law or the circumstances surrounding Molly's death, please visit the following sites:

- www.isba.org/barnews/2016/09/07/molly-s-law-gives-some-wrongful-death-claimants-more-time-sue

- news.wsiu.org/post/gov-rauner-signs-mollys-law#stream/0

- thesouthern.com/news/local/communities/carbondale/governor-signs-molly-s-law-in-southern-illinois-surrounded-by/article_609da033-8075-530b-9f4a-3f182e54f199.html

Death scene investigation protocol:
All death investigations should be investigated
as homicides until proven otherwise.

-STUDYBLUE.COM

PART ONE

The Investigators Speak

CHAPTER ONE

Cold Case Investigation

BY JAMES H. LILLEY
Retired Investigator

First and foremost, we should be aware of, and thankful for, the thousands of men and women in the law enforcement profession who work tirelessly, and often without thanks, every day to solve violent crime. It is often forgotten, and many times ordinary citizens are totally unaware of the sacrifices these men and women make to close a case. They place devotion to duty and service to community above their own family, missing birthdays, Thanksgiving, Christmas and other special occasions with those loved ones in order to pursue a suspect or possible lead.

Investigating a cold case is unique and challenging. It's a crime that remains unsolved over a period of time, often years or decades, leaving family and friends frustrated and often angry over a lack of closure. Why a particular case falls from one of active investigation to a dormant file can vary from lack of viable suspects to absence of real or circumstantial evidence. Yet, there is also the realization that cases can fall inactive due to poor/improper investigative procedures, crime

3

scene contamination, failure to properly identify, collect, preserve and log crime scene evidence and failing to detect and interview suspects and witnesses. Some cases might be marked as closed due to a rush to judgment, careless investigative techniques or unwillingness by investigators to evaluate and pursue leads or accept evidence provided by family, friends or witnesses.

There are also times when investigators are obstructed in their pursuit of a suspect when confronted with uncooperative family members, friends, witnesses and, in some cases, the victim. Reasons for their reluctance to cooperate with investigators can range from fear of reprisal from the suspect to simply not wanting to become involved in the investigation. Then there are entire communities who do not trust law enforcement officers and will not cooperate with investigators, even though their information would solve the crime.

Reopening a cold case presents challenges to investigators from the outset. Certainly, there is no active crime scene for the investigator to view and the length of time the case has been inactive can impact the process of the investigation. Therefore, initially, they will have to rely on the content of the original report, the physical evidence (if still available) collected at the crime scene, photographs of the scene and written or recorded witness statements. Of course, many crime scenes in recent years have been videotaped, which can provide investigators with a much more in-depth look at the setting of the crime.

Reviewing the original report and all written documents relating to a crime is a good first step toward resolving a cold case. Review of the initial report and other documents is not a mere reading of words, but a search for valuable evidence. It's a study of the crime through the eyes of the assigned investigator and attempting to piece together what happened through fresh eyes. Are there valuable statements or evidence that were overlooked? Was an incriminating account given that was somehow missed?

Investigating a cold case should be a very careful study of reports, witness statements (written and recorded), evidence collected (if available to you), and crime scene photographs. In reviewing the deaths of Patrick Rust and Martha Morgan, I found myself going over reports, studying photographs, and listening to recordings again and again. Crime scene photographs were thoroughly studied to try to determine what happened. Documents, especially witness statements, were scanned for evidence relevant to the event. Recordings were replayed, listening to the person's voice and how they reported a death.

The death of U. S. Army Sergeant Patrick Rust is an example of failures and a lack of pursuit of significant evidence, resulting in the case falling into the inactive and eventually cold case files. In this case there were three jurisdictions, the U.S. Army Criminal Investigations Division at Fort Drum, the Watertown, New York Police Department and the Jefferson County, New York Sheriff's Office involved, in some way, in investigating Rust's disappearance and death.

Although the cause of Rust's death was ruled undetermined, I believe more than sufficient evidence was available to classify his death a homicide. Having read and studied information provided to me regarding Sergeant Rust's death, I discovered a number of statements that directly identified probable suspects in his death. For example, a U. S. Army investigator asked a witness if he knew where Patrick Rust might be. The soldier responded, "If I was him and had twenty-seven-thousand dollars, I'd be in Canada, if I wasn't already dead."

This statement seems to very clearly indicate that this witness knows Patrick Rust is dead and he has knowledge as to what happened to Rust. Furthermore, another soldier admitted to his girlfriend that he had taken part in the beating death of someone and aided in hiding the body. Yet, investigators failed to pursue any of those leads. Did the fact that Patrick Rust was last seen alive in a gay bar where he had gone to meet a friend play a role in the failure to close this case?

There is no denying that almost everyone has some degree of personal bias and, unfortunately, these prejudices might influence or sway their approach to a particular event. In this instance I can only ask if personal beliefs or prejudices influenced the manner in which Patrick Rust's death was investigated? To say we should put individual biases aside in this, or any other instance, is easier said than done. Still, investigators owe the Rust family the same degree of professionalism investigating this case, as they would provide to everyone else in the community. As law enforcement officers we take an oath to protect and serve the citizens, in our respective jurisdictions, who call upon us in their times of need. It is our duty to answer their pleas without hesitation or discrimination.

In looking carefully over the information available, I could not find any evidence that Patrick Rust was gay. In fact, there were ample indications that he had a girlfriend and friends from his past believed him to be heterosexual. The fact that he went to a gay bar to meet a friend does not indicate he was leading a secret or gay lifestyle. This case remains open due to the failure by law enforcement agencies to pursue viable leads and suspects.

The death of Martha Morgan in Shreveport is unresolved due to a rush to judgment and the unwillingness of police to reopen the case. Her death was ruled a suicide by the medical examiner and, in spite of evidence to the contrary, he will not reverse his ruling.

From the very beginning, conclusions were reached prior to police arriving on the scene to investigate. Dennis Morgan, Martha's husband, called 9-1-1 stating his wife had committed suicide. The call was dispatched to the initial responding officer as a reported suicide, and the word or police radio code for suicide was repeated over and over before the officer arrived at the scene.

It appears that the initial responding officer had accepted as fact, that Martha Morgan had taken her own life prior to his arrival at the residence. With the suicide thought already firmly in mind, he walked into the Morgan residence and looked at the incident merely as a report taker, not a crime scene investigator. Flags of suspicion were readily visible if investigators had looked closely. Morgan's body was obviously moved, as postmortem lividity was clearly visible on her back, yet she was found face down. Bruising on her face, neck and hands certainly indicated that she had been assaulted prior to her death. Still, the most obvious flag of suspicion was Dennisa and Dennison Morgan pointing a finger directly at their father and saying he had killed their mother. To add validity to their accusation they stated their father was a violent man who had repeatedly abused them as well as their mother and had, on occasion, threatened to kill Martha.

Martha Morgan had a single gunshot wound under her left breast, but there was no bullet hole in the shirt she was wearing when officers arrived on the scene. The medical examiner offered the explanation that she had raised her blouse, held up her left breast and then shot herself. He further stated this was common with large-breasted women who committed suicide.

The weapon used was a Taurus snub-nosed, hammerless, ultra-lite .38 caliber five-shot revolver, and could be fired only in double-action mode. The trigger pull for this particular weapon is twelve to fifteen pounds of pressure. Martha Morgan, who was right-hand dominant, would have had to hold up her left breast with her left hand, hold the gun in her right hand, turn it, squeeze the trigger and fire a straight round with a slight downward angle.

Dr. Thoma, the medical examiner, gave conflicting accounts as to the distance it was from Martha Morgan when it was fired. He has said it was fired from four to five inches away and then stated it was fired from one inch away. He has offered no explanation for the differing rulings on the distance.

In an attempt to get a clearer picture of how Martha Morgan allegedly shot herself, I asked volunteers to assist in reenacting the scenario provided. Eight women participated, five of whom were large-breasted. The weapon used was a Charter Arms .38 caliber, five-shot, snub-nosed revolver, which is smaller than the Taurus.

Attempts to turn the weapon toward the body while utilizing the standard grip proved to be very difficult, and more so for the large-breasted women. At the same time, it was almost impossible to fire the gun in the double-action mode. The attempts to fire the gun caused noticeable movement, thus severely limiting the degree of accuracy. This then raises the question of how Martha Morgan could have fired a single shot straight at her body. When applying pressure to the trigger and holding the gun as it would have had to be held, the weapon began turning to the right. If the weapon had discharged in this position, the bullet would have entered the body at an angle from the right to left side of the body.

All women who volunteered in the attempted reenactment asked the same question. "Why would she raise her blouse?"

One added, "It doesn't make sense."

All said they would not shoot themselves under a breast if they chose to end their life by firearm.

Neither the hands of Martha Morgan nor those of her husband were tested for gunshot residue. Conducting gunshot residue tests on Martha Morgan's hands would either prove that she fired the weapon, or that someone else fired the shot. The reason given by Dr. Thoma for not conducting the gunshot residue tests was the expense involved. This claim is easily refuted as test kits can be purchased for forty-nine dollars from Amazon, and others from various sources for under a hundred dollars; all can be found online.

The autopsy report states there were no injuries on the neck, hands or face of Martha Morgan. Yet, color photographs clearly show bruising to those areas. The police report failed to note these injuries as well, although it is logical to assume that these wounds were not self-inflicted. The crime scene photographs also show a large ball of hair the same color as Martha Morgan's on the floor, but this too is not mentioned in the police report. Dennis Morgan's call to the 9-1-1 operator also raises flags of suspicion. His screams sounded forced and his initial call scripted. His tone remained the same throughout and he spoke in complete sentences, which is very unusual for a man who is supposed to be distressed. He states, "My wife just committed suicide."

If he just discovered her body lying face down, how can he definitively say she killed herself? Shortly thereafter he says, "My God, I don't even see a gun." How did he know she had been shot? These questions were never answered.

Another suspicious aspect of Dennis Morgan's 9-1-1 call was his immediate offering of an alibi for his actions and whereabouts during the day and prior to discovering his wife's body. For a distraught man, his words appeared scripted and far too detailed. And he provided an alibi without being prompted by the 9-1-1 operator. Why?

Another piece of evidence pointing to murder instead of suicide is a letter from the U.S. Department of Justice—Civil Rights Division. Dated August 19, 2011, it stated, "Our preliminary investigation based on our experience leads us to believe that this shooting was a homicide premeditated by Dennis Morgan and not suicide."

The letter continues, "It should be noted that Mr. Dennis Morgan is a public employee, being an inspector for the City of Shreveport, which would further lend credence that it would be a conflict of interest for the City of Shreveport, Louisiana to investigate the shooting, regardless of whether it was a suicide or homicide."

The letter further states, "We are unable to determine, without investigating further, if the ruling of suicide by the Shreveport City Police and Shreveport coroner is a lack of experience, incompetence or cover-up, but certainly we do believe Mrs. Morgan was murdered, based on the preliminary dynamics, witness statements and family history."

Still, with this opinion and all other evidence, the Shreveport Police Department refuses to reopen the case, and the Shreveport district attorney has said he will not prosecute Dennis Morgan.

The above cases show failures and, at times, negligence on the part of those responsible for diligently investigating and bringing to a truthful and unbiased conclusion all crimes brought to their attention. Consequently, these cases lost relevance to the investigators, which ended active pursuit of pertinent evidence and or/leads, and finally they drifted into the cold case files.

Any police officer or investigator, who responds to a reported crime with a predetermined notion as to the circumstances of the event, will not look at the scene with the necessary suspicious eye and inquisitive mind. That can lead to a failure to thoroughly view and see valuable evidence at the scene, and to fail to interview family, friends and witnesses as potential suspects. Any death, not of natural causes, should be carefully investigated as a homicide until proven otherwise.

JAMES H. LILLEY

James Lilley is a former Marine and highly decorated twenty-five-year veteran of the Howard County, Maryland Police Department. Over his career he worked in the Uniformed Patrol Division and the Criminal Investigations Division, investigating crimes from auto theft to burglary, robbery and murder. He also served three years as supervisor of the Forensic Services Section, working with Crime Scene Investigators gathering and processing evidence at various crime scenes.

CHAPTER TWO

The Larsfolk Case

BY JENNIFER PADDON
Private Investigator

As a private investigator, there are few things more tiring and frustrating than working on a cold case and encountering police who are reluctant to cooperate with non-law enforcement professionals because it is still technically classified as an open investigation.

As cyber-sleuthing and the ability for families of unsolved crimes to share their stories and theories becomes more popular and easily accessible via internet tools like social media and podcasts, it's a good time for law enforcement to reassess their guidelines and policies about how they share information in these unresolved cases.

Amateur investigators who wade into cold case investigations for personal interest reasons, or a desire to help, distress family members who seek answers and have managed to gain the pro bono services of professionals in the field of forensics and cold case investigation. Such individuals would benefit greatly from better communication and collaboration with law enforcement agencies and easier access to relevant information.

One case I've worked on comes to mind as a good example of collaboration between myself and an investigating officer, but also serves to illustrate how police departments still hang on tightly to the information they have. In this case, they were not willing to allow me access to the case files and I eventually came to a point where, without their information, I could not move the case forward. Unfortunately, this occurs in situations even where law enforcement has limited, and often inadequate, resources to dedicate to a cold case, yet they are preventing the private investigator from offering their skills and expertise to advance the case by doing some of the legwork that the police department simply may not have the ability to do at the time.

Eric Larsfolk was a fourteen-year-old boy who had recently moved to the rural area of Caledon, Ontario in the summer of 1981. John McCormick Jr. was a fifteen-year-old boy who lived down the road from him on his family's countryside property. According to family members, on August 24, 1981, Eric and John Jr. were hanging around the McCormick property. This was the first time the teenagers had spent time together, though they had already become acquainted with other members of each other's families.

The McCormicks lived on a large piece of land with a house and workshop set back from the road, typical of the many farm properties in the area. A secluded lot sat off to the edge of one part of the property in a wooded area where John McCormick Sr. stowed multiple vehicles. Just past this makeshift storage area was a gravel pit owned by a private company.

By all accounts, Eric was a typical teenage boy in the 1980s. He had recently won a new bicycle which he was very proud of, and there is no known history of him abusing drugs or alcohol. Both Eric's father and older brother described him as a good kid who was happy at home. I was not able to identify any major problems or dysfunction in the home, apart from possibly the normal adjustment that comes along with a recent move to a new city.

John Jr. was a bit of a different story. As many teenage boys did, he was known to have experimented with marijuana, but his home life could be described as quite turbulent. While John Jr.'s mother and sister appear to have been a source of comfort and love for him, his father was an alcoholic with a temper. There are allegations that John Jr. had recently returned from a stay with relatives after his father had beaten him to the point that he required medical attention. In my interviews with family members and neighbors, it is evident that McCormick Sr. had a reputation for being a mean drunk. Eric's older brother had spent some time hanging out at the McCormick house and remembers that John Jr. got a laugh out of pushing his father's buttons, which John Jr.'s sister confirmed.

On the afternoon of August 24, 1981, the boys were having fun driving around some of John Sr.'s old cars that he had stored out back. This was not a problem in and of itself, but John Jr. had a history of driving these cars on the large lawn of the McCormick property and tearing up the grass, which infuriated his father. John Jr.'s mother was at work on this day, and his sister was babysitting for a neighbor.

John's sister, who was also just a teenager at the time, stated to me that when she arrived home, she went looking for the boys. She states that she was immediately worried because John Jr. had a van he was working on, and it was parked in the driveway. She was worried that he would be in trouble for this as his father had previously complained to him about getting oil on the paved driveway. She set out looking around for the boys and they were nowhere to be found, so she reportedly called her mother at work and asked her to come home.

However, I have differing accounts about what happened when John Jr's sister arrived home. While she states there was no one around outside the house, the man whom she had been babysitting for states that were two children in the driveway when he dropped her off. He claims to remember this because he had to keep an eye on where they were while he turned his car around. His wife confirmed this to me as he mentioned it to her when he returned home.

The police arrived at some point that evening and found the field car the boys had been driving out where the old cars were stored close to the area of the gravel pit. It was stopped in the middle of the path with the hood lifted and the doors open. Eric's brother described to me that this particular car was one which required John Jr. to use a screwdriver under the hood to start. It appears as though the boys had stopped the car there for some reason and before they had started it up again, they simply vanished.

As police reports have not been made available to me, it is not entirely clear when the police were called or when they arrived. It is also unclear to me when the Larsfolks were notified as I have been provided with differing accounts from different family members. It appears that Mrs. McCormick contacted the Larsfolks and called the police when she returned home from work. According to Mr. Larsfolk, the police decided to search the gravel pit some time that evening after the sun had set because he recalled, quite vividly, being down on his hands and knees on the ground around the pit while people searched with flashlights.

When I interviewed Mr. Larsfolk about this case in 2008, he said that John Sr. made a curious comment to him that evening. He claims that John Sr. did not appear worried and told Mr. Larsfolk he believed the boys had stowed away in the back of his friend's truck who was at the house earlier that day. To my knowledge, in all other accounts, John Sr. stated to police that he was the only person home until John Jr's sister returned home. This friend John Jr. was referring to is believed to have been a man I will call Greg.

Greg seems to have been quite typical of the type of men John Sr. was friends with, guys he could work on cars with and drink with. John Sr. who was a wealthy man and reportedly did not need to work by this point, spent a good portion of his time hanging out with his friends and drinking. Greg would later be the subject of a very public trial regarding his horrific abuse of an animal. Both Greg and John Sr. are now deceased.

There was no indication that the boys ran away. By all accounts, Eric had a happy home life and no reason to want to disappear. His prized new bicycle was left behind, as were all personal belongings of both boys. To my knowledge, no trace of them has ever been found.

After conducting interviews with family members and neighbors, based on circumstances, it became obvious that if the boys had not left of their own free will, they were most likely harmed by someone who was comfortable being on the property.

The area the boys were in makes it unlikely—and very difficult to believe—that individual(s) with ill intent happened onto the boys on private property and abducted them. Unfortunately, statistics show that if the boys were harmed, it was likely by an acquaintance or family member. As the one person who we know was on the property with the boys, John Sr. was known to have a violent temper, it isn't so hard to imagine a scenario with John Jr. driving around in the car and irritating his father, setting him off and perhaps things got out of hand. The one other person who may have been there, according to statements that Mr. Larsfolk states were made to him on the day the boys went missing, by Mr. McCormick, was also someone with a history of severe violence.

I thought John Sr. and Greg were strong enough suspects that if I were to understand both of them well enough from an investigative perspective, some prime locations as to where the boys could possibly be may be determined. However, all the information I had gathered came from family members, and mostly subjective. I had been told that both of these men were investigated and given polygraphs. I was also told that certain areas and properties owned by John Sr. had been searched. Unfortunately, none of the information the police had regarding investigation of these two men and any searches was never made available to me. I was also told that John Jr.'s sister was given a polygraph test and later hypnotized, but I have never been made aware of the findings.

In an effort to move the case along and find some resolution for the family, I provided the Caledon Ontario Provincial Police (OPP) with my interview notes and my thoughts about areas to be searched for the boys' remains. The officer who was handling the case at the time seemed quite keen on my idea of working backward, figure out who John Sr. and Greg were, and perhaps figure out where they would have taken the boys, if either had been involved in harming them or covering up any harm.

She read my notes and communicated with me when she went to locations I had suggested as possible search sites. I was encouraged that she was willing to listen and act, however communication then ceased. If any proper searches did occur at that point, I was not made aware of them. In this instance, the likely suspects were deceased when I attempted to investigate this case.

As a licensed private investigator, I was offering my services pro bono, but in a situation where even the most basic information needed in a case is unavailable, there is only so much I can do. For example, I was never able to establish an accurate timeline due to conflicting reports from family members and witnesses, and no police reports documenting the activities of the day were ever made available to me.

While the OPP officer listened and seemed to be interested in my advice, this was very limited, such as asking me for information about exactly where Greg's property was at the time the boys went missing and which property in that area was owned by the McCormicks (they owned multiple properties in the area). If I had been able to verify information that I had, or rule some things out, as well as get access to statements from/about the suspects, I might be able to come up with a detailed set of investigative recommendations as I had done for other cases. Perhaps I would not offer anything new or that the police hadn't yet tried, but maybe I will, and it wouldn't cost them a penny.

Pro bono investigators are often happy to donate time to help families find answers. Police departments who lack resources or enough personnel could take advantage of this. Sharing information more openly would save time for the experts, private investigators, and consultants who provide their own time and services for free, and ensure that they have accurate and objective details about the case, which are obviously necessary if the investigator is to provide helpful information. The private investigators or consultants could then proceed appropriately and bring the case back to law enforcement when further relevant and credible information, recommendations, or conclusions are obtained.

Finally, there's the issue of the victim's family. Cooperation between law enforcement and privately hired investigators provide the family and loved ones with confidence that the police are trying everything they can to close the case. Knowing that the case is not sitting in a box on a shelf also provides hope. The reason why myself and many other professionals take on pro bono cases is because the families and victims deserve answers, and everyone deserves justice.

JENNIFER PADDON

Jennifer was a licensed private investigator in Canada for ten years, focusing her practice on unsolved cases and equivocal death analysis. She has been trained in Criminal Investigative Analysis and sexual assault crisis counseling and has spent many years working in the field of psychology.

She is currently completing her MSc in Psychology at the University of Roehampton in London.

Any preconceived theories or notions are dangerous in professional death investigation. In addition to errors of assuming a suicide or natural death other preconceived notions may include deaths, which appear to be drug related and/or domestic violence. One must keep an open mind and not be influenced either by the initial reports or the presentation in the crime scene.

-PRACTICALHOMICIDE.COM

CHAPTER THREE

Politics of Murder & the Challenges of Cold Cases

BY SARAH L. STEIN, Ph.D.
Center of Resolution of Unresolved Crime

From a very early age, the concept of a puzzle was fascinating to me. When I was a child, my parents and I used to put puzzles together as a hobby on family vacations. The task of methodically finding just the right spot for a particular piece was very pleasing to me; it appealed to my desire for order in a chaotic world.

A regular mystery, a case, is not unlike a puzzle. One generally knows the facts, and what the case looks like from the outside. However, it is only when one immerses him or herself into the fragmented pieces of the investigation, the family story, the evidence, the victim's life, and the perpetrator's mind, that those pieces begin to take particular form.

A cold case is similar to rediscovering an old puzzle on a shelf from days past. Perhaps some pieces are missing; perhaps the picture of what the puzzle is supposed to look like is faded, like the memories of the detectives who once worked the investigation. It then falls to a set of fresh eyes to reimagine what that puzzle could look like based on the evidence, and what pieces are needed to complete the puzzle: sometimes, you only need one.

I began my career in cold cases while in college at American University in Washington, D.C., by sort of a fluke. In a criminal justice course, we were asked to research an unsolved case. I chose twelve-year-old Ashley Marie Pond from the FBI's website.

Ashley disappeared on her way to school in Oregon on January 9, 2002. Two months later, on March 8, Ashley's friend, thirteen-year-old Miranda Diane Gaddis, also disappeared on her way to school. The girls lived in the same apartment complex, attended the same middle school, and were on the dance team together.

Just prior to her disappearance, Miranda was interviewed by local news about Ashley. She said that she missed her friend, and hoped she returned safely. One reporter who interviewed Miranda suggested I contact Mr. Ward Weaver III, the girls' neighbor who lived down the street on the route the girls took to school. Mr. Weaver's daughter was friends with both Ashley and Miranda, and both girls had spent time at the Weaver home.

When I reached Mr. Weaver by telephone, I should have quickly realized it was odd that he would speak so extensively to a nineteen-year-old college student, but I thought he was simply trying to be helpful. We spoke for nearly two hours during our first conversation. Mr. Weaver presented himself to be charming, affable, and genuinely concerned about the girls' well-being. During one conversation when he told me that Ashley's online handle was BlueAngel89 (which later proved to be untrue), I remember getting chills. I remember thinking, what a macabre screen name for a twelve-year-old. In my mind, I began to wonder if that's how Weaver saw her. . .as a blue angel.

I began researching Weaver and discovered that his father was on death row in San Quentin prison for abducting, sexually assaulting, and murdering a young woman after killing her fiancé. When I questioned Weaver about this, his mask of pleasant congeniality slipped off—he became enraged, screaming at me that he was nothing like his father. After this, our communications ceased, though I would receive several calls over the summer on the eighth and ninth of each month around the time Ashley and Miranda disappeared. I am certain those were from Weaver.

In August 2002, Weaver sexually assaulted his son's girlfriend, and attempted to murder her. She was able to escape, and the attack provided law enforcement the probable cause they needed to search Weaver's property. In the end, they recovered Ashley's body from a barrel under a concrete slab Weaver had installed, and they found Miranda's crumpled remains shoved into a box in a shed on the back of his property.

I had unwittingly been speaking to a murderer.

As I watched law enforcement on the news tear apart Weaver's backyard and the residents in Ashley and Miranda's neighborhood erect a shrine around Weaver's home with banners, stuffed animals, and flowers, I decided to commit myself to doing everything I could to prevent this type of crime from happening to any other person, and help resolve those tragedies that had already occurred.

After the dust settled in the investigation, it became evident that the deaths of these children might have been avoided had social service and law enforcement agencies acted earlier in an appropriate manner. It was then when I began to grasp that while cases may eventually be resolved, there is plenty more that could be done proactively to expedite the process and perhaps prevent another tragedy. Simply put, we can do more. About a year later, I was well into my studies at American University with my self-designed undergraduate degree, The Victimology of Pedophilia.

During that same time, on June 9, 2003, the remains of Molly Bish were identified in rural western Massachusetts. I recalled having read about Molly's case in high school. On June 27, 2000, Molly vanished from her lifeguarding post at Comins Pond in Warren, Massachusetts. The crime scene revealed very little. Molly's shoes, radio, open first aid kit, and belongings were there, but Molly was gone.

Due in part to Molly's father John being a probation officer, and given the mysterious nature of her disappearance, the search for Molly became the largest ever for a missing person in the Commonwealth of Massachusetts. Molly's Mother, Magi, had described a mysterious man in a white vehicle watching her and Molly on June 26, 2000, and other witnesses had reported seeing a similar white vehicle in the vicinity of Comins Pond on the morning of Molly's disappearance. Following initial theories of Molly having run away, having drowned, or leaving her post with friends, the man in the white car theory became the most feasible, and the hunt was on.

Despite thousands of hours of searching by law enforcement, retired officer Timothy McGuigan with the assistance of acquaintance Ricky Boudreau cracked the case. They found Molly's bathing suit five miles from Comins Pond on the side of a mountain known locally as Whiskey Hill.

In the end, only twenty-six of Molly's bones were recovered and she was buried on August 2, 2003, her twentieth birthday.

I left a note on the family's website, offering whatever help I could. In December 2003, John Bish, Molly's father, called and invited me to Massachusetts to meet his family and consult on Molly's case.

When I arrived in Warren, John took me to Comins Pond. There were yellow ribbons still tied in memory of Molly, which fluttered in the lonely breeze. The weight of the trauma and sadness around the site resonated in my spirit. I felt a shift in my heart and a profound desire to find the answer as to what became of Molly, and who was responsible. John gingerly untied a ribbon, handed it to me and said, "We really can't afford to pay you anything, but I hope you will always remember Molly."

Years later, after obtaining my master's in Forensic Science and Ph.D. in Criminal Justice, and working tirelessly on Molly's case and many others, the time had come to reconceptualize my career.

Up until 2018, I had worked in two capacities: as a civilian cold case consult for law enforcement agencies, and as a consultant and advocate for families who had become frustrated with the criminal justice system.

As a law enforcement consultant, I was granted access to case files, and submit victimology, suspectology, timeline, forensic, interview and interrogation, and investigative plan reports for follow up. In my second capacity as a consultant for families, I would host tip campaigns, go to meetings between law enforcement and families, raise public awareness about cases, make suggestions for follow-up, and pass along relevant information to law enforcement.

While I hoped that these two avenues of my work allowed for some temporary measure of relief for law enforcement and families, the cold case epidemic in the United States continued to grow while criminal justice and law enforcement systems remained stagnant despite the obvious need for macro-level policy examination and reform.

In addition, many of the cases I consulted on were never acted upon given that I had no official capacity or jurisdiction to affect any resolution; it was up to law enforcement.

These two revelations, the fact that our criminal justice system is fractured, if not completely broken, in the way we deal with cold cases, and despite my efforts, the families I had been serving still remained at a disadvantage because of this, led me to want to affect change on a macro-level. Of course, individual cases are tragic—unfathomable.

That being said, it's only when families and activists band together, when many voices become one, that change becomes possible. Without unity in purpose, the hope of tackling the cold case epidemic in this country quickly fades.

It's essential to stop focusing on individual cases and glamorizing them on channels like Investigation Discovery with the sole purpose of salacious entertainment value. Instead, we need to focus on critical examination of the macro-level issues that led us to this crisis and enact policies that could make a difference.

The sole culprit behind our cold case dilemma is politics—the politics of murder. In the following sections I will examine the politics of the media, of elected officials, and of law enforcement, and how collectively they impact the resolution of cold cases.

During my Ph.D., I derived the idea for my dissertation research from the case of Molly Bish. Molly was a beautiful, blonde-haired, blue-eyed, all-American girl. The media frenzy surrounding her case was unfathomable. Looking at other cases, such as JonBenét Ramsey and Elizabeth Smart, I began to theorize that perhaps this was not a coincidence.

Missing White Woman Syndrome, the concept that attractive, caucasian women who are reported missing receive disproportionate media attention compared to their racial counterparts, has existed for quite some time. However, I believed, and still believe, that the issue goes deeper than race, that some other element is at play.

After examining approximately six hundred missing person cases and all associated media, my research supported my theory that as a western, primarily Christian nation, we have been unconsciously indoctrinated via art, movies, advertisements, etc., to view blonde-haired, blue-eyed, caucasian females as archetypal symbols of innocence. That is, when a perceived innocent victim is snatched, undoubtedly a media circus, and therefore a political circus, will ensue.

As I advanced my career in criminal justice, the standards by which a victim and their family members were evaluated for priority became apparent. If you are white, wealthy, well-educated, have never done anything deemed wrong or unsavory by society in your life, and have some measure of influence in the political arena, chances are that if you or a loved one goes missing or is murdered, your investigation will be given top priority and with ample resources. If you are a person of color, not wealthy, perhaps didn't have the same opportunities for education, and you don't have any political pull, odds are that the public will not be as outraged, the media will not be as involved, law enforcement will not be given as many resources as they need to help you and your family, and the arrest and prosecution of a perpetrator are far less likely.

In addition to those politics, which are horrifying enough, there is the age-old regime of winning political elections via fear. Since the civil rights era, politicians ranging from those who are vying for district attorney all the way up to the presidency of the United States of America have figured out that crime—and fear of crime—is a great tool for drumming up votes. Come election time, if a candidate for district attorney can drag out names like Molly Bish as a cautionary tale for how easily an innocent child can be murdered, or a presidential candidate can tout the drug and gang epidemics as the root of all America's evils, so long as those candidates have a halfway intelligent proposal for combating or preventing those crimes from infiltrating safe American neighborhoods, they will win.

Therefore, one could argue that solving these crimes is actually bad for the business of politics. Preying on the public's fears is more entertaining and is a much easier campaign to run versus running on integrity, values, and a proven track record of success.

Finally, there is the politics of law enforcement. Allow me to preface this section by saying that the vast majority of those who I've encountered in law enforcement have been dedicated professionals. In most instances, the women and men who tackle cold cases are ethical, intelligent, and respectful people. For most of them, as it is for me, these are not simply cases. The victims and their families become part of the fabric of our lives, they become our family. In that sense, while law enforcement and consultants like me can never fully understand the anguish experienced by a victim and his or her family, we do feel many of the same emotions: frustration, impatience, anger, grief, and a heavy conscience that is always asking, what if we could do more?

However, the bureaucratic structure of most law enforcement agencies—and associated politics within the ranks—is a significant hindrance to the resolution of cold cases. Not everyone in the field of law enforcement is an effective reviewer of cold cases. These cases require months, if not years, of critical examination, tenacious follow-up, and intuitive creativity. The bureaucratic structure of policing in the United States was not built on thinking outside the box. Instead, it is based on law and order, policies and procedures, and retribution for those who dare to stretch the envelope or suggest a new investigative strategy.

Some of the most successful cold case endeavors in this country resulted from law enforcement agencies carefully selecting outside consultants with varying backgrounds to review their cases, and to be followed up on by sworn personnel. Therefore, it would seem logical to expand this practice.

Cold cases usually can't be neatly resolved. They're disorganized, messy, and often the truth that emerges from the investigation will be stranger than fiction. The right set of eyes for the task of reviewing a cold case may not be within the confines of a police department, and the recognition of this fact by law enforcement personnel is a critical first step in the effort to reduce the cold case backlog.

According to The Murder Accountability Project, between the years of 1965 and 2017, we have amassed around 300,000 unsolved murders in the United States alone. In addition, there are about 40,000 unidentified dead lying in morgues. These numbers are staggering. We can and must do more. We simply must.

As this section of the book is entitled The Investigators Speak, I offer the following advice for law enforcement. Our law enforcement community is struggling. Since 9/11, resources have been pulled from almost every aspect of law enforcement to fund our war on terrorism, and to date, conditions have not improved. Manpower is tight, budgets are even tighter. I recommend getting creative with your cold cases—do not be afraid to think outside the box.

For example, the tip campaign is the most successful method I've ever used. Using college interns and volunteers, I host tip campaigns to solicit information from the public. Typically, a local hotel donates a conference room, a press release is distributed about two weeks in advance, a dedicated email account for tips is set up, and we ask folks to come in on the day of the event and provide their information.

In the case of Molly Bish, the tip campaign I held in 2014, resulted in the best person of interest in the investigation, to my knowledge. In fact, multiple witnesses came forward that day, all naming the same individual. From hosting tip campaigns, two themes became apparent: people had previously reported the information and no one from law enforcement followed up, or people were too afraid to talk to police and felt more comfortable with a civilian.

I ask that law enforcement remember two critical things:

1. According to Dr. Robert Keppel, the investigator lauded for his work in the Theodore Bundy and Gary Ridgway cases, in 95% of cold cases, the perpetrator will be named in the case file in the first thirty days of the investigation.

2. In cold cases, the people you most likely need information from may have unsavory backgrounds and be reluctant to talk to police.

These two facts support why civilian teams of cold case reviewers have been effective. In hindsight, when reviewing cases for police, I was often able to identify the point where an investigation became derailed. Perhaps a detective got tunnel vision, or a certain lead wasn't followed up on. This is not to criticize the skills of law enforcement. It is simply to say that in the heat of an active investigation, it is easy to become misdirected. An impartial reviewer, perhaps one with a different vocation or personal background, may be able to provide an unbiased observation.

Secondly, do not be afraid to use the public in your quest to solve these cases. Social media campaigns, cold case playing cards in prison, and public tip campaigns are all viable options. Your imagination is the only limit.

For families, my recommendation is to not lose hope. While the circumstances under which your loved one was taken might lead you to believe that you're not in control of your life, your fate, or the destiny of your loved one's investigation, do not lose hope.

- There is much that you can control, but deciding how best to use your energy and financial resources is often quite difficult.

- Communicate frequently with law enforcement representatives assigned to your case. If you haven't been given a victim or witness advocate, ask for one. They are useful as a communication tool between your family and the police.

- Coordinate with law enforcement about talking to the media. While you want to publicize your loved one's investigation to the best of your ability, you also don't want to damage the integrity of the case should a perpetrator ever go to trial.

- Set up GoFundMe campaigns for donations, social media pages and groups, and gather as much information as you can to provide to the police.

- There are many support groups available to you, such as Survivors of Homicide, Citizens Against Homicide, etc.

- Finally, approach your local politicians. Make sure they know you are not going away until your loved one's case is resolved.

If you do all the above and nothing changes, call an outside consultant who may be able to assist you further.

Please know that you are not alone, and there are many people willing to fight both alongside you, and for you. And remember the words of Mahatma Gandhi: "When I despair, I remember that all through history the way of truth and love have always won. There have been tyrants and murderers, and for a time, they can seem invincible, but in the end, they always fall. Think of it—always."

DR. SARAH L. STEIN

Dr. Sarah L. Stein is a consultant and co-founder for The Center for the Resolution of Unresolved Crime (www.thecruc.com).

Dr. Stein was awarded her Ph.D. in Criminal Justice in 2012. Her dissertation was entitled The Cultural Complex of Innocence: An Examination of the Social and Media Construction of Missing White Woman Syndrome.

Dr. Stein received her master's in Forensic Science with a concentration in Advanced Investigation and a certificate in Computer Forensics in 2007, and her Bachelor's in 2004, was a self-designed major entitled The Victimology of Pedophilia.

Dr. Stein has co-authored two texts on cold cases, and published several articles related to the topic. Dr. Stein's areas of expertise include cold cases and missing persons; she consults regularly for law enforcement agencies and families in the United States and internationally.

CHAPTER FOUR

The Killing of Kaitlyn Arquette

BY PATRICIA A. CARISTO
Private Investigator

The Kaitlyn Arquette killing in Albuquerque, initially dispatched as an "accident without injuries," on July 16, 1989, became classified as a random drive-by shooting incident. Months later, the case stagnated.

In January 1990, the Arquette case got new attention because of a Crime Stoppers tip identifying four hispanic youths as the shooters. All four were arrested and a full investigation was conducted by Albuquerque homicide detectives.

It may be important to consider that the tip about the hispanic shooters came in to police just days after the Albuquerque Journal ran a story reporting that the Vietnamese subjects who were close to Kait's boyfriend were not being investigated, and pointed out the stagnant investigation of the shooting death of the eighteen-year-old girl. The Bernalillo County district attorney twice dropped the charges against the hispanic males for insufficient evidence, and gave a statement to the media recommending that Albuquerque Police Department (APD) look into the Vietnamese angle.

When an APD homicide supervisor was quoted to say, "We are very interested in looking at the new angle," the family had hope, even though this new angle about the Vietnamese suspicious behavior had been reported by the family just days after Kait died. In fact, APD did not investigate the new angle—they dropped off the case, telling Good Morning America they were never going to make any other arrests.

In 1991, frustrated by the lack of action in the case, Lois Duncan Arquette, Kait's mom and a well-respected author, wrote a book about the case called, "Who Killed My Daughter?" Both the book and the case became high-profile and were featured on many well-known TV news and commentary shows.

My involvement in the investigation began in 1992, when I was a private investigator doing work for an Albuquerque personal injury attorney. I was contracted to investigate the drive-by shooting aspects of her death. The initial assignment was to obtain copies of police reports in order to get the statement which specified that the shots that killed Kait had been fired from a vehicle. Not being able to establish that fact from the available police reports, the attorney requested we do a scene reconstruction to establish that the shots that killed Kaitlyn had been fired from a vehicle.

Working with a certified accident reconstructionist, I did the requisite preliminary work while the reconstructionist used the details to come to a determination that the shooter had to be in a vehicle traveling at approximately forty miles per hour when the bullets struck the victim in the head while she was driving her car. This information was submitted to the personal injury attorney.

In the meantime, the insurance claim-related case, which required the family to file a civil lawsuit against the uninsured motorist policy, was not pursued; the family did not want to be viewed as profiting from Kait's death. The investigation for the civil attorney ended, but because I was able to retain the large volume of investigation materials we had put together, I decided to use the case as a teaching tool for my new apprentice investigators program on how to work a case in real-time and as a cold case.

In 1994, while watching the Sally Jesse Raphael show featuring psychics working on unsolved cases around the nation, Lois Duncan Arquette was one of several mothers who were presenting frustration about their unsolved cases. As I listened to Mrs. Arquette present what she had been told by the Albuquerque Police Department, she made no mention of the fact that an APD officer encountered a young man standing next to Kait's car with her wounded body inside. This man was at least a witness, and because of a police history of violent actions toward women, was a viable suspect. Believing the information I had uncovered could be important, I called the show's info line and left a summary of what I knew about the Arquette case. A few days later, an attorney representing the Arquette family contacted me to ask the source of the information I had provided. I detailed the information I had extracted from initial police reports but hadn't been included in the homicide investigation report.

The family engaged me to collaborate with this attorney, who was working with insurance investigators looking into a Vietnamese staged auto accident operation in California. Pursuing information the family had learned, Kait and her Vietnamese boyfriend had recently traveled to California, and were involved in a staged auto accident. Insurance payments had been deposited into Kait's checking account.

The California and New Mexico Vietnamese links were added to our database, and the scope of our private investigation expanded. As I processed the new names and data, I began to see links to other killings and other crimes. With help, I construct a specialized database to manage all the information.

The complexities of the Arquette case caused me to adopt a new investigative work process, a case data-analysis approach I learned as an intelligence analyst with the New Mexico Governor's organized crime unit. I developed a case template using three columns: an outline for key datapoints, word-for-word entry of the actual case documents, and questions that arise as data is being entered.

I created a separate template for each of the ten initial case documents: APD's Incident Report, the Supplemental Report from the off-duty APD detective who had come across the scene, other APD officer Supplementals, the Criminalistics Report, reports submitted by Albuquerque Fire and Rescue and Albuquerque Ambulance. The data and questions compiled from those ten templates formed the starting point of a formal private investigation. The method informs me as to what is known, what needs to be known, and what information and sources are needed to follow up.

This process revealed that the APD homicide investigation into the Arquette murder was incomplete, inconsistent, and inaccurate. It pointed to persons not fully interviewed or evaluated, and what was done and not done in the days, weeks, and months after the killing.

Within the first ninety days of APD's investigation of the murder, APD had contacted and/or interviewed only sixteen people, six of which were interviews of witnesses to a threat made by a local medical doctor against a female coworker in which he alluded to the Arquette killing, which were eliminated immediately as a possibility.

APD did not identify nor do a follow-up interview of the man found standing next to Kait's car when the off-duty detective came on scene.

APD did follow up on a piece of paper with directions found on the floor of Kait's car and made contact with a woman Kait had visited that night. They were told that Kait was troubled and trying to avoid her Vietnamese boyfriend. Kait was shot just minutes after leaving this home. After learning that this woman had provided inaccurate information, been involved in a questionable cutting-stabbing injury the day of Kait's funeral, and had taken Kait's job days after the murder, APD investigators, however, never re-interviewed her.

APD did contact Kait's live-in Vietnamese boyfriend at the apartment they shared, and took into evidence a note said to have been written by Kait but, in fact, was not. On the day of Kait's funeral, that boyfriend was found stabbed in the stomach in the U.S. Air Force dorm room of a Vietnamese friend. The stabbing was classified as a self-inflicted wound.

Despite information from Kait's parents about her and her boyfriend's involvement in staged auto accidents in California, APD did not follow up. APD also declined to take information from Kait's personal counselor, who tried to report that Kait was telling her that she was afraid of the boyfriend and his friends, that they were involved in questionable behavior, and she was going to report them to police.

APD also took information from Kait's landlord that Kait sought safety from the Vietnamese boyfriend and his friends, and the landlord had ordered the boyfriend out of the apartment, but they did not use the information as a working lead.

APD investigators dismissed damage to the rear of the victim's vehicle as "old," because no corresponding debris was found where her car came to rest. They did not expand the scope of the scene to include information they were learning. An APD criminalistics investigator who dropped by the scene made some observations that on-scene investigators used as fact but produced no written report. APD reported that only minimal bullet fragments were found, no bullets or casings. One detective later stated that he and the team discussed the possibility of a second larger-caliber weapon, however, there is no mention of this in the investigation reports.

APD reported that no fingerprints were found on the vehicle. There should have been prints from the driver, medical responders, etc. Did they mean no workable prints? Or did they not process the car for prints?

The scene processed by APD did not include information from residents of a home just around the corner from where Kait's car was found. They told APD that after hearing shots fired, they looked out of their house to see a VW Bug occupied by at least two persons coming from the area where Kait's car was on the sidewalk and up against a pole. The VW Bug pulled into the parking lot of the business next to their home, made an abrupt U-turn, turned off the headlights, and drove away in the opposite direction. APD reports list the location as a dirt lot, when in fact it was a working body shop and mobile home transport business.

Later in the private investigation, after a fire at this location and the tenants had moved out, I obtained permission from the property owners to allow my apprentice investigators and myself to inspect the buildings. During this walk-through, we looked through some of the burned debris. One item was a partially burned personal check that I realized had been written by the woman Kait had visited just before she was shot. We were able to link that VW Bug, which was listed in APD reports as a small car, to the man found next to Kait's car.

The Criminalists Report placed the location of shots fired at a location they refer to as the area of the greatest concentration of glass. However, their crime scene photos show no indication of visible glass nor any evidence markers in the photos. APD reports say they took into evidence a red and white can of Budweiser beer from the area where the concentration of glass was reported. APD reported that partial prints were developed on the can, however the can and the prints were never connected nor compared with the man found at Kait's scene, who had recently been arrested for illegally firing a weapon while in possession of Budweiser beer cans.

Records show the Arquette case began when an APD off-duty detective, who was enroute to headquarters after working a shooting case a few miles away, arrived in the area at about 2300 hours. He wrote in his supplemental report:

> I was driving west on Lomas Blvd. Ne from Interstate 25 south. As I approached Arno NE, I could see two cars on the north sidewalk at Tom's Motors, 400 Lomas Blvd. NE and I thought it was probably people looking at cars. As I passed the vehicles, I noticed the red car was against the light pole and then I thought it was probably an accident. The lights were on and the car was facing east on the north side of the street. I asked the dispatcher if an accident had been reported and the response was negative. I made a U-turn on Lomas at Arno NE to investigate the situation. I was met by a man who stated he had just stopped to see what was going on.

In response to this radio inquiry, APD dispatched a uniformed officer to the scene. According to my analysis of the radio logs obtained some years later, that officer arrived at 2302 hours—within fifty seconds of being dispatched. That officer's incident report states:

> On last date writer was dispatched to Arno and Lomas in reference to a possible accident without injuries in which Ofc. Merriman had pulled on to. Upon arrival Ofc. Merriman and writer approached the vehicle which was partially upon the curb facing eastbound in the westbound lanes. writer heard moaning as ofc. Merriman opened the passenger door and located the victim later identified as Kaitlyn Arquette slumped over in the passenger seat with blood rushing from what appeared to be the mouth face and head area. the listed interviewed subject (Paul Apodaca) stated he was westbound on Lomas when he observed the listed vehicle but did not see the vehicle jump the curb which hit a telephone pole.

The significant inconsistencies in APD's Arquette investigation began with the conflicting information from the first two officers on the scene. When interviewed by me, each contradicted the other about what occurred in the first moments at the scene. Each said the other was lying about who did, or did not, make contact with the man found at the scene. Neither would state why the man was permitted to leave the scene without being properly identified or interviewed.

When I later identified, found, and interviewed this man, his information was in variance with both officers. In addition to the conflicting information from these three persons, was the information I learned when I interviewed the two crew members of Albuquerque

Ambulance, who were the first to treat the victim inside her car at the scene when they arrived between 2302-2312 hours. The EMT on the ambulance crew told me:

> That was the information that came over dispatch, that is why we were surprised that we didn't see PD at the scene. There was no one at the scene when they arrived—they missed the scene because they saw no vehicles in the street to indicate an accident, made the U-turn and then saw the victim's car against the pole. There were no police on scene. There was no man standing at the car. Police started arriving after AAS arrived.

The Albuquerque Fire Department report noted they arrived on scene at 2306 hours, and found the victim unresponsive with massive head trauma, lying across the front seat of the vehicle. They noted that the patient appears to have a gunshot wound to left temple area with wounds above left eye with bone fragments and possible brain tissue showing. Second gunshot wound to left cheek. Category I, gunshot wound to head.

It was the fire department who made the determination of a gunshot injury. The APD officers at the scene did not recognize the holes in the driver's passenger door/window as bullet holes. At that point, additional APD personnel were requested at the scene.

Early in my investigation, I was certain that the questions I raised had been asked and answered by APD homicide detectives. I later learned that wasn't so. The homicide investigation report does not include much of the information I detailed here. It also became clear that APD'S casework had been compartmentalized in such a way that all the information was not made available to all investigators working on the case.

The private investigation process developed information about suspected drug shipping at both Kait's place of employment and that of her Vietnamese boyfriend. The woman who last saw Kait alive was reported to also be involved in dealing drugs from her car outside Kait's place of employment. The business location where the VW Bug made its U-turn and fled was determined to be a chop shop and possible drug distribution point. APD officers were reported to hang out at this location. Several officers linked to this location and to Kait's case were arrested for criminal activities.

Deaths were connected to this location and to APD officers. I posited theories about what may have happened, listing reasons for the suspicion and the reasons against. Because of the lack of specific and comparable facts developed by APD in the early stages of the case, it was difficult to come to a verifiable hypothesis.

All the information that had been developed and would develop in the next couple years was provided to law enforcement. It was, and is, my thinking that it should be law enforcement who solves Kait's case. I turned the information over to APD investigators. We met with all levels of law enforcement persons, experts/consultants, OMI professionals, defense attorneys, other investigators, etc. During our private investigation we interviewed more than one hundred fifty persons—including the girlfriend Kait had visited, several of the

Vietnamese friends of her boyfriend, the next-door neighbor who told police he saw Kait leaving her apartment that night and was followed by a VW Bug (which APD dismissed as invalid information).

We made formal contacts to twenty-five reps of government, city and federal law enforcement, prosecutors, etc. We encouraged all to look at the connections we had developed linking Kait's case to others. Many agencies did request copies of the case and were provided with the APD homicide investigation report. However, that report did not contain the materials about the scene. Rather, it mostly reported on the investigation into the hispanic suspects.

I met with the new supervisor of the APD cold case unit who agreed to review our private investigation materials. At a follow-up meeting, I was advised that her detectives had assured her there are no possible suspects other than the men they had arrested. Also, because Kait's mother's book had maligned an impeccable department, APD would not accept any information from family or our reps.

The APD cold case unit disbanded, and then recreated in 2005. When I met with the new supervisor, he said he would not discuss the Vietnamese angle as it had no merit. However, he was interested in the man found at the scene who had a long record of violent assaults upon women. The supervisor was preparing to interview the man, who was then incarcerated for rape, when the cold case investigator was suddenly transferred to the pedophile unit. The man at Kait's scene has not been interviewed, and APD's cold case unit dropped off Kait's case yet again. Detective Steve Gallegos, the initial homicide

48

investigator, did listen and was willing to dialogue with me about the case, but nothing came of our discussions.

In recent years, the case has been reviewed by Sheryl McCollum, Institute Director, Cold Case Investigative Research Institute (CCIRI) at Bauder College in Atlanta. She and her team came to Albuquerque, and did a scene reconstruction and case review. They consider Kait's case to be worthy of follow up.

A documentary team is also looking at the Arquette case, and I have provided them with all case information. Interestingly, when CCIRI visited Albuquerque, and reconstructed the paths of travel on the day of the killing, they found a witness who came to our office for an interview. Although the information did not reveal anything new, it did reinforce our investigation results.

Our process developed twenty cases in common with persons connected to Kait's case, sixteen Vietnamese subjects of interest, four other possible suspects, and three persons of interest. We created a chart of those in control of the case. In conclusion, in a case considered stagnant, we found and developed viable investigative leads that weren't identified or pursued by APD, as follows:

1. We identified a viable suspect and vehicle as potential shooter (not included in APD's investigation);

2. We determined that key persons were not formally interviewed and information from/about them was not pursued by APD;

3. We coordinated information that showed an organized criminal

enterprise: multi-state arson and staged auto accident fraud in which Kaitlyn and her Vietnamese boyfriend and his associates were involved and told to keep quiet about, and organized criminal behavior in computer chip theft, drug trafficking, chop shop operations, and extensive student loan fraud;

4. We identified instances of potential witness intimidation which weren't looked at by APD;

5. We identified numerous errors and omissions in the crime scene and investigation reports, and found what appears to be a manipulation of the police investigation efforts that may have resulted in false arrest of hispanic suspects;

6. We discovered links between persons in the Arquette case to multiple other cases involving killings and other crimes;

7. We worked on information about possible shipping of narcotics between businesses linked to persons in the case;

8. We found links to persons and cases involving drugs and connected to police informants;

9. We submitted our information and requested involvement of several law enforcement jurisdictions;

10. We developed a working database of case materials.

Our investigation concluded that the shooting was not random. Kaitlyn Arquette was deliberately targeted and killed because she represented a threat to the shooter(s) and/or those who ordered the killing. APD omitted, compartmentalized, and manipulated aspects of the investigation which caused the case to remain unsolved. Instances of manipulation of case information occurred early in the case, and continues even after the case is considered closed.

APD has concluded the hispanic suspects are the shooters and declines further actions.

PATRICIA A. CARISTO

Pat Caristo has been a licensed, working private investigator since 1985, and the principle of National Investigations Agency of New Mexico. A sworn investigator for the Philadelphia Police Department from 1967 through 1973, Pat and her family relocated to Albuquerque, where she became the first woman detective at the University of New Mexico Police Department, and then a special agent with the New Mexico Organized Crime Prevention Commission.

In 1985, Pat became the owner/investigator of NIA/NM and ultimately specialized in unsolved homicide investigations.

In early 2000, as an instructor for UNM's Continuing Education Division, Pat developed and still teaches a sixteen-hour adult education class, Introduction to Private Investigation. In 2012, the class was listed 15th among the top 25 PI training programs.

Pat is the founder and working director of the NIA/NM's Resource Center for Victims of Violent Death, a nonprofit agency advocating for those dealing in the aftermath of the violent death, founded in honor of Kaitlyn Arquette and so many other victims taken by violence. Kait, an 18-year-old girl found shot twice in the head while inside her red sedan on a Sunday night in July 1989, just minutes after leaving the home of a new friend, is still waiting for her case to be solved and for her killer(s) to be brought to justice. Pat remains committed to answering a mother's question: *Who Killed My Daughter?*

What is interesting is how much power homicide
detectives have and how much respect.

-THEO JAMES

PART TWO

The Survivors Speak

CHAPTER FIVE

Sgt. Patrick S. Rust

BY JUDY RUST
Patrick's mother

In January 2007, my son Patrick was assigned to the U.S. Army 10th Mountain Division headquartered at Fort Drum in Watertown, New York. He was twenty-four years old and had just returned from a deployment to Afghanistan. He returned to the base  in March following a leave. Patrick was born and raised in the area—he didn't have a car or driver's license.

On March 12, Patrick called and told me he was going to move off base into an apartment with a fellow soldier who was looking for a roommate. He said he'd known the other soldier for about fifteen months and had discussed the move while they were in Afghanistan. On March 14, he moved into apartment #4 at 156 Sterling Street in Watertown.

I didn't hear anything from or about Patrick until March 20, when I got a call from Watertown police stating that soldiers from Patrick's unit had been to the station the previous day to report him missing. Because the soldiers were not relatives, they couldn't file the report. My ex-husband and I would have to come in.

When I got to the police station, I learned that Patrick had been missing since the night of March 15. Why it took four days to notify me, I have no idea. I knew one thing for certain: Patrick loved the Army and had just reenlisted. He would never go AWOL. I was sure something bad had happened.

For the next six months while the Watertown police and Army Criminal Investigation Division conducted investigations, members of Patrick's unit and I attempted to locate him, too. We put up posters and made pleas for information through the local newspaper and TV stations. Some sightings of Patrick were reported, but none of them panned out. The days, weeks, and then months passed with no word.

On September 16, six months to the day Patrick went missing, I got the news no mother should ever receive: skeletal remains had been found in a field about three miles outside of Watertown. They were Patrick's. My son was dead.

When his remains were found, the Jefferson County Sheriff's Office (JCSO) and Army CID began investigating his death. The Armed Forces Medical Examiner System conducted an autopsy. Due to condition of the remains, a toxicology test could not be conducted, and his manner of death was listed as undetermined.

I learned some basic information about the night Patrick died. He was last seen in a Watertown bar called Clueless, a known gay and lesbian bar. He entered alone around 9:30 p.m. While there, an old high school classmate came in with his boyfriend, another Fort Drum soldier. The three talked quite a bit and went outside together a few times to smoke. At around 1 a.m., Patrick left the bar, apparently exiting unseen via the front door, which was used only for deliveries.

Why was Patrick in Clueless that night? Where did he go when he left the bar? Who was he with? These were questions I was sure the JCSO or CID would find answers to. Wrong!

The JCSO detective in charge of the case placed the investigation in inactive status in 2008, due to a lack of leads. CID closed its case shortly afterward.

I wanted answers as to how and why my son died. The fact that JCSO and CID were apparently giving up was not acceptable to me. I called the detective several times and he never answered nor returned my calls. I finally called the sheriff and complained, which infuriated the detective.

A friend and I located the boyfriend of Patrick's classmate who had been at Clueless that night. As one of the last people known to have seen Patrick alive, it seemed that he'd be someone the detective would want to talk with. He had been discharged as a soldier and was working at the local Target store in Watertown. I called the detective and provided this information. He now had a workable lead, and I later learned he went to the Target store. When he found the potential witness wasn't there, he left a card with the manager and a message to call him. The call never came, and that was the end of his efforts.

In June 2010, with no active investigation in progress, I retained Forensic Consulting Specialties (FCS) in Syracuse to investigate the case on my behalf. What they found was very disturbing to me. Some of their findings are listed below in their partially redacted report. See what you think.

> Civilian investigators appear to have acted under the belief that Patrick was an open homosexual and a regular customer at Clueless, a known gay and lesbian bar. His fellow soldiers had learned of his alternate lifestyle, and his fear of being outed led to a drug and alcohol binge that contributed to his accidental death.

> However, interviews with several people including both the manager and the owner of Clueless, show that Patrick had never been in Clueless prior to the night of March 15, 2007. Other than the police theory, no witnesses have been found who report that Patrick was gay. On the contrary, he was seeing two women on or about the time of his death. Patrick's friends and acquaintances state that he was not gay, and had several relationships with members of the opposite sex.

> There is nothing in any of the reports or other documents reviewed, or independent interviews of Patrick's family, friends and acquaintances, to indicate that Patrick was on a drug binge in the days immediately prior to his disappearance and death. In fact, other than a statement given by Kristyn (redacted), the wife of Spc. Scott (redacted), that her husband claimed to have sold Patrick cocaine the day Patrick disappeared, and an allegation by the classmate's boyfriend that Patrick mentioned cocaine that night in Clueless, we have found no evidence that Patrick used drugs at all. He was drinking, however. He had a documented history of alcohol abuse and had received related counseling by the Army.

Another area of concern is the apparent lack of investigation by the JCSO. FCS has spoken with many of the persons who were in a position to have information about Patrick's activities around the time of his disappearance, who claim they have never been interviewed or contacted by sheriff's investigators.

In addition, Judy Rust opened a tip line in April 2010. A tipster called and reported that she had spoken with a woman in August 2007, who said her boyfriend had been with Patrick the night he disappeared. The JCSO was informed of the tip and promised to come by to get the information. A year and a half later, they have yet to respond. While this is only a tip that might prove to be nothing, it seems that in a death investigation, it warrants at least being checked out.

FCS also did an analysis of Patrick's cellphone records. As far as I know, this is something JCSO and CID failed to do. I believe the calls provide information that should have been followed up on. The FCS analysis and comments are below. Patrick's cell phone records do not reflect text messages. They do show the following regarding calls made and received.

MARCH 15

At 17:43 there was an outgoing call of six seconds–probably a hang up–to (redacted), the cell phone of Spc. Dylan (redacted), a friend of Scott (redacted), who was a friend of Patrick's and an alleged drug dealer.

At 17:46 there was another outgoing call to Dylan's number. This one was 144 seconds in duration. During both calls Patrick was presumably at the apartment with his roommate.

At 18:32 there was a 48 second incoming call from Dylan's number.

At 18:36 there was a six second outgoing call to Dylan, followed by a 46 second outgoing call at 18:39, at which time Patrick and his roommate were presumably in route to or at the mall. When CID questioned Dylan about these calls he said he and Scott were together the afternoon of the 15th. However, Scott didn't have his own cell phone with him and used Dylan's phone for contact with Patrick. Dylan's recollection was that the reason for the calls was that Patrick was looking for a ride somewhere.

This explanation is suspect for a couple reasons. According to Kristyn (redacted), Scott's wife, Scott was never without his cell phone; it was virtually a part of his body. She also alleges that she and Scott were more or less split up at that time. She and their daughter were living in their apartment in Syracuse and he was staying on base most of the time. On or about March 16, Scott told her that if anyone asked his whereabouts on the night of the 15th, she was to say he was with her at the apartment in Syracuse. When she asked what was going on, he explained that he had sold Patrick cocaine on the 15th. Patrick had gone missing and he didn't want to get tangled up in the investigation.

And since Patrick was with his roommate and had transportation at the time of these calls, he had no reason to seek a ride unless it was to do something else later in the evening. According to a JCSO document, during a March 2008 phone call Dylan told JCSO Detective (redacted) that when he spoke with CID he omitted to say that Scott provided Patrick with drugs on the 15th. He said he withheld that information because he feared he'd be arrested and his military time extended.

Sandwiched between the 18:32 and 18:36 calls was a 363 second incoming call from Patrick's father, Rod Rust, and Rod's girlfriend Debbie Smith. Smith later stated to FCS that this call was to confirm plans for the trio to go to Syracuse after Patrick got off duty on the 16th and spend the weekend celebrating St. Patrick's Day and Rod's birthday. She said that during the call Patrick said he was on his way to the Square in downtown Watertown to meet with a soldier who was having marital problems. She also said that based on Patrick's breathing she had the impression he was walking at the time.

Based on the pattern of calls and the fact that Scott was on the outs with his wife, it is possible, if not likely, that Patrick was planning to meet Scott. But at the time of the call it is believed that Patrick was with his roommate on the way to or at the mall, not walking to the City Square. If Debbie is correct, perhaps Patrick was walking around in the mall and the meeting he referred to was for later that evening.

Dylan admitted to CID that he picked Patrick up at about 7:55 when he saw him walking in the City Square and gave him a ride the three blocks to his apartment. He didn't mention Scott being with him and implied the ride was not pre-planned. However, a Watertown PD report states that Scott and Dylan were together when Patrick was picked up.

There was a 481 second outgoing call to Debbie/Rod at 18:50. Debbie was unable to provide any specific details of that call.

There was no further phone activity until 22:39, when Patrick received an incoming call of 44 seconds from the cell phone of PL. It is believed that Patrick Rust was at Clueless at that time and had encountered PL, a former school classmate. The two hadn't seen each other for approximately five years. PL was a known homosexual and frequent patron at Clueless along with his current love interest and roommate, Sgt. Travis (redacted). Patrick and PL exchanged phone numbers and this call may have been a test call to confirm the number, or an accidental dial when the number was programmed into PL's phone.

MARCH 16

There were three more incoming calls from PL in the early hours of March 16:

1:03 a.m. for 21 seconds;

1:04:07 a.m. for 11 seconds; and

1:04:33 a.m. for 206 seconds

The first two calls may have been hang ups. However, the third call lasted for over three minutes and may well have involved either a conversation between Patrick and PL, or a lengthy voice mail message.

The records show the next phone activity was two outgoing calls from Patrick to PL. The first call was at 1:36:32 for six seconds and was an apparent hang up. That was immediately followed at 1:36:39 by a call lasting 148 seconds. It is believed that the second call resulted in a conversation or a voicemail message being left.

Although Patrick's exact whereabouts at the time of these calls is unknown, it can be reasonably assumed that he was still okay and not in any difficulty. But as far as is known, PL has never been formally questioned by any law enforcement agency or given a written sworn statement regarding the circumstances behind any of these calls, or the content of any conversations or voicemail messages. And PL, who has since joined the Army and is stationed at Fort Drum, has refused to meet or speak with FCS investigators.

One of the mysteries of this case is what caused Patrick to visit Clueless for the first time on the night of March 15/16, the same night he died. It seems logical that at some point during the conversations between Rust and PL that night, PL would have inquired as to what brought his old classmate to Clueless, an establishment with a distinct reputation. It seems very unlikely that after not having seen each other for several years, PL, the regular customer, wouldn't have asked that question of the newcomer.

The phone records also call into question the actions of Patrick's roommate because of what they don't show. In sworn written statements made to CID investigators, he said he awoke around 5 a.m. on March 16, 2007, and Patrick was not at the apartment. He said he called Patrick's cell phone but was transferred to his voicemail. He then sent a text message to his supervisor, SSgt. Saa, saying Patrick hadn't come home and would not be at the 7:30 a.m. formation.

However, Patrick's phone records show no phone activity from the 1:36:39 outgoing call to PL until an incoming call from his roommate at 6:22 a.m. – approximately an hour and twenty minutes *after* he texted Saa stating that Patrick would not be at formation.

Why there is no record of the call the roommate claims to have made at around 5:00 a.m. is not known. And there is no information indicating that the roommate was ever interviewed by civilian law enforcement, or that the CID inquired about this apparent discrepancy.

In SSgt. (redacted) sworn written statement to CID investigators, he acknowledged accessing Patrick's voicemail account on or about March 18, 2007. He played back Patrick's messages and heard at least one that he thought was suspicious. Whether he deleted any or all the messages, or possibly recorded them, is unknown.

Other than the initial report of Patrick's disappearance to the Watertown PD on March 19, 2007, there are no records or reports available that indicate SSgt. (redacted) was interviewed by civilian law enforcement regarding this case.

On December 15, 2015, I had a heart issue my doctor attributed to broken heart syndrome brought on because of Patrick's death and the stress of fighting the system to get answers. As a result, I had to keep away from the investigation for a couple of years. I've recovered and now I'm back to continue the battle.

I believe there are discrepancies between law enforcement's version of Patrick's death and the FCS findings. I'm now on my third JCSO detective handling the investigation. As with the previous two, he promised a lot, yet I've seen no action so far. Although it is very frustrating, I'm not going to give up until I know how and why my son died.

JUDY RUST, Patrick's mother

Each murder is one too many.

-JURGEN HABERMAN

CHAPTER SIX

Theresa Corley

BY GERRI HOUDE
Theresa's sister

We have often wondered how one person could have such bad luck. How could you nearly save yourself from a bad situation only to be found naked and murdered on the side of a highway?

Perhaps telling yourself, "Just one foot in front of the other, I am almost home, less than a mile to go, a walk I've done on many occasions."

The only difference this time being the traumatizing event that found my sister Theresa walking home at 5 a.m.

Could a girl escape from an apartment in which she was sexually assaulted, only to be picked up by a different set of individuals? Different men, but all part of the same small circle, connected through drugs?

It was Monday, December 4, 1978. My nineteen-year-old sister Theresa told my mother she would not need a ride home from work. Being a school night, she promised not to be too late.

Friends were gathering for a birthday party at a bar called the Train Stop in Franklin, Massachusetts. Most of the people were from the Franklin-Bellingham area. Most were college students, and many worked at Penthouse Sales, as Theresa did, a jute factory that made shoes, rugs, pocketbooks etc.

Present at the party were children of Franklin cops, Theresa's work supervisor, her current boyfriend, and some of her best friends. People who would later profess to have loved her, yet despite clear intoxication, they let her walk out into the night alone.

The party started at the Train Stop, and Theresa drank more than usual, for whatever reason. This information was learned over the last three years from my conversations with several people who observed Theresa that night.

In piecing the events together, I have trouble understanding how a murder deemed solvable by private detectives, has not been solved in almost forty years. According to Theresa's boyfriend, a guy I'll call Ed, Theresa left the bar angry that night, perhaps due to an alcohol-induced argument. Ed said they had argued over something stupid, though he couldn't remember exactly what. It could have been that Ed's ex-girlfriend had shown up and he paid some attention to her. He recalled that Theresa's last words to him were, "I'll show you."

She asked a high school girlfriend to drive her home, but the girl wasn't ready to leave. A guy then tried to hit on Theresa, and she treated him rudely, embarrassing him. Regardless of the cause, it was reported that Theresa decided to walk home. It is known that she was picked up by three or four men in a car on the premise that they would take her home. Instead, they took her to a party at an apartment in nearby Franklin. It is unknown if Theresa got into the car willingly or was forced.

I am unaware of what happened in that apartment between 11 p.m. and 4 a.m. One partygoer told my private investigator he let Theresa sleep in his bed and said, "No one touched her."

During a heated meeting with my family at the Norfolk County district attorney's office, a detective from Massachusetts (MA) State Police said Theresa was "held down by two men while the third was assaulting her, he just did not finish."

Theresa either fought off the assailants or they let her leave when she resisted. One of the assailants reportedly told an acquaintance that Theresa was "orgasming when suddenly she reached up and scratched my face." Theresa apparently then left the apartment in a hurry, putting on one of her own shoes and one shoe belonging to one of the men. It's my theory that the men may have realized how upset Theresa was, and went to look for her so she would not or could not talk.

The investigation revealed that after leaving the apartment, Theresa was given rides by two separate dairy farm truck drivers. The second driver stated he left her at the entry of the Bellingham Police station. Theresa had indicated to him she had been sexually assaulted. Even though he had a teenage daughter himself, the driver did not see fit to make sure Theresa got help. His story checked out, so his DNA was never obtained.

A few days later, Theresa's naked body was found in a gully on 495 North. She had been strangled. A few days after that, the State Police conducted a roadblock and interviewed commuters on their way to work. They learned Theresa had been seen on foot less than a mile from home. Why she ended up dead and at whose hand remained a mystery.

I was seventeen years old when my sister was murdered. I have little recall of the actual investigation. I do remember my sister Linda went to the local police with any information she heard. She thought the leads she provided would be followed-up on. We know now that may not have been the case, or, if information was cataloged and added to the file, it has since gone missing.

In 2015, questions about Theresa's death remained unanswered. With my own children grown, the time seemed right to inquire as to the status of the investigation, and what could be done to bring the case to some conclusion. My approach was to talk with previous investigators, retired police officers, detectives, Theresa's friends, coworkers and people who were at the Train Stop that night. I knew I would reopen old wounds, especially with Theresa's friends and some of my siblings. What I didn't anticipate was the animosity from some people, especially her boyfriend Ed. It was sheer anger.

According to a previous girlfriend, Ed could be violent. I found speaking with her to be interesting. During our very first conversation Ed's previous girlfriend told me she was questioned by the police due to a dream she had about Theresa—a dream that something bad was going to happen to her. The previous girlfriend said Theresa and Ed argued because of Ed talking to her that night at the Train Stop. When she had met with Ed a couple days prior to the party, she told him, "Nothing good can come from being with Theresa." As far as I know, she hasn't been interviewed again.

Another part of my search was starting a Facebook page, "Justice for Theresa Corley Bellingham MA 1978." I began to receive messages from various individuals claiming to have information or theories about what happened to my sister. A common rumor was that a cop was either directly involved in her murder or diverted information that would help to pinpoint the actual perpetrator(s). The main suspect was a drug dealer who was known to throw drug parties that included several of the persons of interest. In addition to the drug angle, many of these guys were related by blood or marriage.

On December 8, just before police arrived on the scene of where Theresa's body was found, the drug dealer entered the Bellingham Police station. Extensive notes were made by the dispatcher. I later learned the logbook in which he wrote those detailed notes could not be located just days after the body was found. The dealer's family was well-to-do and had business connections to the police department. I spoke with the owner of a police hangout where the drug dealer also frequented. He told me the dealer would sometimes want to talk about Theresa when he was drinking or high. The owner encouraged the dealer to talk and get it off his chest. But then the dealer would either catch himself and say, "If I talk, it will all come undone," or if he was with friends, they would stop him from talking. He died in Florida in 2008, I believe from complications of his drug issues.

What did he know about Theresa's murder that he was afraid to talk about? Whatever it was went with him to his grave.

And what about the disappearance of the dispatcher's notes and the relationship between the dealer's family and the police? Was it just a coincidence, or something more sinister?

When I inquired to the Norfolk County DA's office regarding the Bellingham Police reports, I was told they lacked detail, and "That was how it was back then."

As my sister Linda did years ago, I shared any information I came up with on my own or through my private investigators, with the State Police and called their office regularly to get updates on their investigation. It wasn't long before I learned I was being too aggressive. I was told, "You know the squeaky wheel gets the grease. But in this case, you are being over the top." That was followed up with, "Where did you get your junior detective badge?"

Despite the insults, I continued looking for answers and within a couple of months I discovered details about Theresa's murder I had never heard before. Surprisingly, to this day the detectives don't seem at all fazed by some of the things I learned. Another surprise for me is that I did not expect former or current investigators to try to shut me out, and not be direct with me about the status of the investigation, but they did.

I felt and still feel that some witnesses might be more comfortable talking to a family member rather than the police. So, I continue to seek people out. I have encouraged those I speak with to call detectives themselves. Some did, but reported back that they left messages that were never returned and had to keep calling.

Over the years, the number of suspects grew. Things got further complicated in 2012, when a person came to the Bellingham Police, claiming that one of his friends confessed to two acquaintances that he had killed Theresa. I enlisted the help of statement analyst Peter Hyatt to review that statement. Peter concluded the statement had no merit.

From other information I received, there was a possibility the son of a Franklin Police officer might have been present in the apartment when the sexual assault took place. However, I have never been able to confirm that rumor.

In 2015, when I began my investigation, the detectives hoped to rely on forensic evidence, a degraded semen sample found on Theresa's jeans. At that time, we were waiting for technology to catch up to be able to test a degraded sample. A vaginal swab done at autopsy was lost in a fire according to State Police investigators. At the local level, they were told the swab was lost in a flood. The story evolved to, "It was a fire that became a flood." Yet my research failed to find any documented fires at any state police crime lab. I've noticed a very distinct change in the way I was treated as my questions became more specific. At this point, I've filed a Freedom of Information Act request to get a definitive answer as to what happened to the vaginal swabs. I want to be reassured they were not simply misplaced.

In December 2017, forensic testing revealed a Y-STR profile obtained from Theresa's jeans. We were initially told the results would be entered into Combined DNA Index System, only to be told later that a veteran assistant district attorney had made a mistake in giving us that information.

We were next informed that there was no database for Y-STR profiles, yet with recent advances in other types of testing, M-VAC for one, and law enforcement agencies seeking DNA comparisons through genetic testing databases. We wonder about the accuracy of that information and can't figure out why, or if, we are being misled.

We typically do not get updates unless we call the advocate assigned to us, who relays questions and answers back and forth. Of course, frustration ensues with the fear that eventually they will not be actively working on a case they insist is open, especially when it is my desire to bring in an outside source who could dedicate themselves entirely to Theresa's case.

At one point, the first assistant DA made verbal threats to me, stating, "This office is looking for something to charge you with." He accused me of harassing suspects by asking them about Theresa, and what happened to her. Most of the persons I have encountered have a history of violence against women. For one person in particular, I learned this from a newspaper article in which he was arrested for trying to strangle his girlfriend, despite a restraining order.

As a family, we do not want to interfere with an ongoing police investigation. Yet, we are at a place where we feel we can't win. Law enforcement says Theresa's case is an open murder investigation, yet have shown little or no interest in solving it for thirty-seven years. For the past three years, I've asked that new eyes be allowed to review the case file—an investigator of the family's choosing—and my request has been denied.

So, we wait and wonder. Will we ever get the full story and the truth about what happened to that girl who almost made it home in December 1978?

GERRI HOUDE, Theresa's sister

No one is above the law. Not a politician, not
a priest, not a criminal, not a police officer.
We are all accountable for our actions.

-ANTONIO VILLARAIGOSA.

CHAPTER SEVEN

Morgan Jennifer Ingram

BY TONI INGRAM
Morgan's mom

In 2011, our nineteen-year-old daughter Morgan became the target of a stalker. How long it had been going on, we don't really know. First her car was keyed and damaged to the tune of two thousand dollars. We didn't think of this as stalking, but it was.

Months later, the stalking activity escalated to startling taps on her bedroom and bathroom windows, and then frightening pounding against another bathroom window as Morgan got into the shower. Peeping Tom, harassment, eavesdropping. Those are all the things that came into our minds at the time. Who was doing this? The first sheriff's deputies called it stalking, but in their report, they wrote only that it was suspicious activity.

Our daughter was thrust into a dangerous situation, with a sick twisted individual actively stalking her and a sheriff's department that pretended to care, but did not.

Morgan was a student at Colorado Mountain College, with a love of philosophy, a passion for dance, and a constant appreciation for all forms of art. She was an extremely gifted artist and loving person who saw and gave beauty to others through her talent in photography. Forever in tune with nature, Morgan loved animals, music, playing piano, and singing.

Our youngest child, she was still living with us while attending college. Because most of the incidents of the stalking occurred at and around our home, my husband and I were listed in the police reports as victims of the same stalking case. But Morgan was the main target. As parents, we were extremely concerned, and then as the stalking escalated, we were scared to death for our daughter's safety.

We reported incidents of stalking over seventy times in four months. We had photographic, video and eyewitness proof of the stalker. We kept a detailed timeline of the incidents. The main suspect is named over and over in the police reports, emails and text messages, with his accomplice, who was somewhat protected (and redacted from the reports), as she was still a minor. According to the deputies, they both had extensive criminal records, which we would never see because their records were sealed.

On the morning of December 2, 2011, we found our daughter dead in her bed. This was only four days before she was scheduled to give her on-camera statement to the sheriff for an impending arrest of the suspect in her stalking case. The detectives told the suspects this detail just days before her murder.

Her room was the scene of an obvious struggle. Her panic button, which was hidden by her bed and would summon her father with a baseball bat if pushed, had been torn off and tossed across the room. Her cellphone, which she always kept in bed next to her as she slept, was found under her bathroom door. Her pants were unbuttoned and unzipped. Her bottom bedsheet was missing, as were her pillowcases and the pajamas she had worn to bed. There was blood on her forehead, lips and teeth. Her nose looked smashed. She had a fat lip, tangled hair, abrasions on the top and bottom of her right hand, and three torn nails on her right hand. Amazingly, her hands were frozen in rigor, signing the first and last letters of the stalking suspect's name! The sheriff's office dismissed all this evidence and called her a slob. Her death was ruled to be from natural causes.

I believe the sheriff's office needed our daughter's death to be something other than a homicide to avoid an investigation. They took no evidence, only Morgan's personal items, camera, computer, cell phone, iPod, and one old diary. The camera came back missing all the memory chips, and the computer's hard drive had been altered while in police custody. They were investigating the victim, not the suspects.

They had stated it was a suspicious death because Morgan died during their active investigation into her felony stalking complaint, only two nights after the detective assigned to her case warned us that he believed the stalking was going to escalate; and he was assigning additional patrols of our home. Morgan was not sick. At the time of her death, she was a healthy twenty-year-old female. Because she had no obvious reason to die suddenly, her body was sent for an autopsy.

For the first nine months after her death, the pathologist insisted her death was from natural causes. He said it was from a blood disorder she was never diagnosed with. He admitted he found no evidence that she died from this disorder, but insisted it was a diagnosis of exclusion and ignored her own doctors.

Records were kept from us, and it would be years before outside experts determined that Morgan's body had been moved postmortem. Bodies do not move on their own after they are dead. The sheriff knew about that yet covered it up. It was a staged crime scene. For reasons we may never know, they began a cover-up of Morgan's death, and have since fought to keep her case from ever being investigated.

In another shock, the autopsy timestamps show a window of time of only eleven minutes to perform the autopsy and document evidence on Morgan's body and clothes. A detective at the scene saw bodily fluids on her chest (it's in the police reports), but none were noted during autopsy. Bodily fluids can't be there, and then not there. More important, eleven minutes is not enough time to fill out the standard paperwork, let alone investigate anything.

We know they drew blood and gastric fluid, but the pathologist admitted he never tested for foreign DNA under her torn nails, never did a rape kit, never took samples of her organs, never ran tests for chloroform or any other substance that could have rendered her temporarily unconscious. He insisted that the sheriff's office would have had to authorize him to run those tests, and they did not. He listed a healing burn on the inside of her arm on the autopsy diagram. But years later, after receiving the crime scene photos, this was clearly seen as an injection point with a bite mark around it. This, plus many more false statements, were written down by the forensic pathologist to cover up our daughter's murder.

When we wanted answers, we didn't get them. The sheriff's office closed her felony stalking investigation five months after her murder. We were told no more Morgan, no more investigation, case closed.

So, what does this mean? If a stalker kills you before he or she is arrested, then there will be no investigation into your murder? No justice? Eliminate the victim, and a stalker-murderer gets away with it? In Garfield County, Colorado, this is what happened.

We later found out from proper scientific interpretation of the toxicology reports that Morgan died from a massive overdose from a sexual assault drug. It couldn't have been ingested—it had to have been injected, as it was ten times the amount that would have killed her. The full amount was injected into her bloodstream through the injection point seen on her forearm. This was known in the weeks after her death but was covered up until another forensic expert explained it to us.

It was later discovered Morgan had six other sexual assault drugs in her gastric contents that never made it into her blood, and she was dead when they were put there. None of those drugs were in our house and Morgan didn't have access to them. Those drugs were brought in and taken away with the murderer.

Later, we were fortunate to receive a pro bono second opinion by a highly respected medical examiner from another county. At that time, he confirmed our daughter had been murdered. We contacted the county pathologist, the detective, and the coroner to explain that they had gotten her manner of death wrong. Instead of investigating the evidence, I was threatened by the pathologist that if I didn't stop asking questions and having other forensic experts contact him, he would change Morgan's manner of death to suicide. Nine months after her murder he made good on his promise, and changed her manner of death from natural causes, which was false, to suicide, which was also false. These two erroneous manners of death determinations allowed the sheriff his excuse to announce that he would never investigate our daughter's murder.

As a further shock, two years after Morgan's murder, when we finally were able to get a copy of the police reports, there were only seven incident reports out of over sixty reported incidents that were written by the deputies. Only one mentioned stalking. The others stated suspicious activity, misdemeanor trespass, or harassment. They completely covered up the number of incidents and severity of the stalking and other crimes.

All the physical, scientific, and medical facts in our daughter's case point to murder, yet the sheriff refuses to allow an investigation. The district attorney informed us that the sheriff's office botched her case so badly, that she didn't think she could ever get a conviction.

Morgan was the victim of a horrendous felony stalking. Although the stalking was reported to the sheriff's department on numerous occasions and a detective assigned to her case, it was an extremely ineffective investigation which ended in her coldblooded murder.

I believe it was a premeditated murder, and there is absolutely no doubt in my mind that she deserved an investigation into her death—not a cover-up of her murder, which is what happened. The stalker—whom she identified with her last dying breath—and his accomplices walk free today.

Morgan needs to have her story told. How can other stalking victims feel hope if our twenty-year-old daughter can be stalked for four months, murdered, and then have law enforcement cover it up? Where is the accountability? Don't they care that a stalker-murderer is free to do it again?

The State of Colorado has no mechanism to file a complaint against a sheriff. They are free to do as they please and make up any story they want. The sheer volume of physical evidence we've been able to gather proving foul play, this homicide and the blind eye by law enforcement needs to be in the hands of an agency who has the power to investigate the sheriff. We cannot do this. How can the State of Colorado allow one of their sheriff's departments to exhibit acts of corruption, and the state will not even investigate them?

I've said many times before that when there is a suspicious crime scene, there needs to be a qualified, certified, and trained expert in crime scene investigation working independently of law enforcement, as the National Association of Medical Examiners states. When the coroner's office is only fed false information by law enforcement, then how can the manner of death be correct? This is a good way for murderers to walk free, and the local, state and national death statistics to become completely skewed.

There's an extremely large number of cold case homicides in the State of Colorado because of the antiquated laws governing coroners dating back to the horse and buggy days, and Morgan's isn't even one of them because her manner of death was initially ruled to be from natural causes. After experts told us this was not true, I would not drop it, and kept asking questions. I was told to stop, or else. When I didn't, I was punished by them changing the manner of death to suicide. Does that sound like they were searching for the truth? Do you agree with me that the entire investigation was a farce?

Since our daughter's murder, I have become a victim advocate working to raise awareness and push for better laws and education about stalking. We need more training and education for law enforcement. Law enforcement cannot be above the law. They need to be held accountable. They are supposed to uphold the law, not distort or turn their backs on it.

Stalking is a pervasive and serious threat. The way Morgan's case has been swept under the rug is horrifying. Almost all stalking victims who contact me say they can't rely on law enforcement to protect them. They no longer trust law enforcement, and feel they are all alone. They are scared and don't know what to do. They don't want to become another murder statistic like our daughter. They tell me their local law enforcement doesn't take them seriously. They don't believe them. Their neighbors often think they are paranoid, and on and on. This is so wrong. Stalking needs to be taken seriously by everyone.

David Beatty is the executive director of Justice Solutions, Inc. and formerly served as the Director of Public Policy for the National Victim Center. Mr. Beatty states, "Too few victims are willing to turn to the law, because they are worried that their complaints won't be taken seriously." This is indefensible because in almost every stalking case that turns violent, the warning signs were already there.

This is what happened in Morgan's case. The sheriff knew who the suspect was, but never arrested him. They told us and Morgan to hold off getting a protection order, in order to give them enough time to catch him in the act, which, of course, never happened and never would happen because of the inadequate stalking protocol they were using. It is sad, yet true. If Morgan had received a protection order, then the next time she saw her stalker watching or following her, she could have had him arrested. It may or may not have stopped him, but it would have been a lot better than doing nothing.

Seven months after Morgan's murder I started a website called morgansstalking.com. I have a blog on that site which, to date, has had over seven million readers from over 115 countries around the world.

Many readers are or have been victims of stalking, and have written to me about their experience. On the blog, I've shared the timeline of Morgan's stalking starting on day one, morganingram.com.

We're sure there are people who know who was involved and know exactly what happened in Morgan's death. We urgently needed somewhere for people to leave tips. Thankfully, Northern Colorado Crime Stoppers stepped in to help:

https://nococrimestoppers.com/morgan-ingram-unsolved-case/

They posted a reward poster online in the hope that it will bring in tips to help solve Morgan's case, since the sheriff will not accept any tips. He turns potential tipsters away by stating there is no active investigation—the case is closed.

Our family will never give up on our fight for justice for Morgan. When she was taken from us, we were left with a huge hole in our heart that will never heal. Until there is accountability for her murder, there can never be closure for us.

TONI INGRAM, Morgan's mom

CHAPTER EIGHT

Andy Atkinson

BY GARLAND ATKINSON
Andy's dad

My only child, Garland Andrew "Andy" Atkinson, along with his girlfriend Cheryl Henry, who was raped, were murdered on August 22, 1990, in Houston. Their deaths were dubbed the Lovers Lane Murders.

All through school, Andy had lived with his mother, grandmother and great-grandmother in North Carolina. I had tried to get him to move to Texas, but he was not interested in relocating. I did get him to come down for a couple weeks during the summer when school was out. He was always ready to get back to his friends after those couple of weeks, though.

In spring 1990, Andy called and said he was coming to Texas to start school at the University of Houston in September. Wow. That made my day. He went to work at Gold's Gym and started hanging out at some sports bars that catered to his age group. This is when he met Cheryl, who was home from college. They hit it off and started dating.

On that fateful night they went to Mama's Bayou Café along with Cheryl's sister, Shane. But what had started out as a night of fun turned into an unimaginable tragedy.

Andy would have turned twenty-two on September 6. I planned to celebrate his birthday with him; instead, I was burying him. I know Cheryl's family experienced that same indescribable pain and loss.

Here is what is believed to have happened. The suspects followed Cheryl and Andy from the club and approached them after they had parked. Blood was found in the car on the passenger side, which shows that Cheryl was attacked while still in the car. They were taken from the car and Andy was tied to a tree where he was later murdered. Cheryl was taken into a field a hundred yards or so from where Andy was killed. There she was brutally raped and murdered.

One of the most difficult things for me to handle in this scenario is that the detectives concluded that Cheryl was killed first. Which means Andy heard Cheryl being raped and then killed, knew he was next and there was nothing he could do. The horror he must have experienced is incomprehensible to me.

When Andy arrived in Texas, he stayed with my mother, who was a nurse. The day after the murders, she called and said Andy hadn't come home the previous night. She also said Cheryl's family had called, saying Cheryl had not returned home, either. I was concerned, but told her they were both over twenty-one, and might have driven down to Galveston and spent the night.

My mother called again later that day. This time she told me that Andy's car had been located, but Cheryl and Andy had not been found. I felt like a horse had kicked me in the stomach. I immediately drove to where the car had been found, and Cheryl's body discovered. Andy was still missing. I remember it being very hot with bugs swarming, making it all even more unbearable.

The search for Andy was suspended when night fell. A Houston police officer was posted to secure the scene until the search could resume at daybreak. Andy's body was found the next morning, tied to a tree with his throat slashed.

You probably don't think anything this horrible will ever happen to you. But it can happen to anyone at any time.

The lead detective told me every individual who was questioned was asked to provide a blood sample for DNA testing. All but one did. This particular individual was a suspect with evidence against him. However, the police could not force him to give a blood sample.

In 2000, the investigator came to get my signature, agreeing to post a fifty-thousand-dollar cash reward. The impetus for this was that local television and Crime Stoppers wanted to announce it to mark the tenth anniversary of the murders. The investigator also said he had submitted an affidavit to a judge, requesting a court order for the suspect to submit a blood sample for testing. The order was granted, but his DNA did not match that gathered from Cheryl's body. The investigator must have seen my disappointment, because he then said the only thing it proved was that this person didn't rape Cheryl. But until proven differently, he believed this guy was involved in the murders. There were other things that happened during this period of time in the way of evidence that I am unable to share at present.

I was contacted by Gene Cervantes of Citizens Against Homicide in California. He introduced me to Denny Griffin of Crime Wire, who also had an interest in the case. Gene and his group were instrumental in getting America's Most Wanted involved. They used Cheryl and Andy's murders as their featured case in 2011. An investigator told me the show generated a lot of leads, though unfortunately none of them panned out. Also, according to him, the composite sketch of the rapist provided by the first victim could fit thousands.

In 2011, DNA taken from Cheryl's body was matched with the rape that occurred six weeks earlier in June. The first victim survived, yet Cheryl's throat was slashed.

At this point, the first cold case squad took over the case. With new detectives and the DNA evidence, I was hoping for progress. Cheryl's father, Bob Henry, and I scheduled a meeting with the Assistant Chief of Police, George Buenick. When we walked into his office, there was a captain, lieutenant and three other homicide detectives there with him. I explained that over the twenty-one years since the murders, I had talked with a lot of people, including the detective initially assigned to the case, and we had discussed facts I felt could be important to the investigation, including possible suspects and persons of interest. Buenick looked at the others in the room and asked if they had heard about this information, and they all said "No."

How could they not know, when much of the information had come from one of their own detectives? These weren't just rumors—they were facts. Yet, they claimed they knew nothing about them. Something just wasn't adding up.

One of the detectives, who I don't recall ever seeing before, said, "Mr. Atkinson, I can tell you that HPD homicide has spent more money and man-hours on this case than any case in the history of Houston homicide."

I just looked at him and replied, "And?" I thought, we are talking about the time and money that was spent for you to do your job. I don't accept that either, Mister Detective, Sir.

Over the next six years following that meeting, I was never contacted by homicide detectives with news or updates. It wasn't until 2017, when a new cold case squad took over, that I was contacted and interviewed by a new detective leading the investigation. One of her first comments gave me a better feeling. She told me that there was more than one person involved with the crime. I always knew there was more than one person involved, yet the first cold case squad repeatedly said they felt only one person was involved. Now there has been a familial DNA match, as well. The new squad and lead investigator gave us hope that we were getting closer.

I've heard of several cold cases that have been cleared or resolved in the past few months with people being arrested. New scientific developments that are identifying these animals must cause Andy and Cheryl's killers some unease. They have gotten away with it for twenty-eight years, but they aren't out of the woods yet.

Losing your child to this sort of crime is terrible enough. Going twenty-eight years without some form of resolution compounds the pain, and I find it totally unacceptable. I don't think anyone would find it acceptable.

These were two young people who had their whole lives in front of them. They never harmed anyone or did anything to have their lives end so abruptly, and in such a brutal manner. Their surviving family members are the forgotten victims of these crimes. Their lives have been shattered and the toll Andy's death has taken on his mother has been devastating.

As for me, my heart aches. I will never see Andy grow into a man in his own right. And I'll never be a grandfather.

These murders cry out for accountability. The people who did the killings must be identified, tried and if convicted, put to death. There is no place for them on this earth. Nothing can bring Andy back. But knowing who killed him and dealing with them harshly, will at least provide some peace and closure.

There are links to the Lover's Lane Murders of Cheryl Henry and Garland "Andy" Atkinson where you can find information I have not disclosed here regarding leads received by the detectives and photos. I ask everyone to read the story. If anyone, especially in the Houston area, has any information, please contact Detective C. Shorten with the cold case squad of the Houston Police Department. She is the only detective in twenty-eight years to give us some positive feelings about resolving the cases of our murdered children.

I'll close with this: These bastards will have to answer for their crimes, be it here or in front of God Himself. I just pray that I will live long enough to see justice served here on earth.

GARLAND ATKINSON, Andy's father

Clearance doesn't equal conviction: It's just the term that police use to describe cases that end with an arrest, or in which a culprit is otherwise identified without the possibility of arrest—if the suspect has died, for example.

-NPR.org

CHAPTER NINE

Ronald Wayne Anderson & Lt. Dan Anderson

BY PHYLLIS ANDERSON COOK
Ron's sister and Dan's daughter

In September 1967, my brother Ronald Wayne Anderson, died under suspicious circumstances, yet his death was ruled a suicide. It was a decision I was never able to accept.

Ronnie was only seventeen, and such a loving and caring young man. Life hadn't been good to him, as he contracted polio when he was three, so he was never able to run, play, or do activities that healthy kids do. He was three years younger than me,

UNSOLVED HOMICIDE
FATHER AND SON MURDERED
RONALD WAYNE ANDERSON 09/26/1967
LT. DAN ANDERSON 04/18/2003
Gulfport, MS

and me being the only girl, I babied him most of his childhood.

In summer 1965, Ronnie was having issues with our stepdad, so he moved to Gulfport, Mississippi, to live with our father. What was to be a new beginning for him turned out to be a living hell.

On September 25, 1967, I was out with some friends when I got this gut-grabbing feeling that something was wrong with Ronnie. He had recently moved into an apartment, sharing expenses with a friend who was a year or so older. I felt as though Ronnie was hurt or needed me somehow. I immediately asked my friend, who was driving, if he would pull over at the next pay phone so I could call my dad. When Dad answered, I asked if Ronnie was okay, explaining my concern. He said yes, as far as he knew everything was fine.

I asked Daddy if he would go tell Ronnie I wanted him to come visit me for a while because I missed him so. The next morning Daddy took Ronnie some money and new shoes. He had to wear a brace inserted into the heel of one shoe because it was two sizes smaller due to the polio. I was to pick him up that afternoon.

I got up early that morning to run a few errands. When I returned home, my stepdad had left a note on my front door that read, "Phyllis, call your mother soon as possible, we have some bad news for you."

I rushed to call my mom, and my aunt Miller answered. I asked, "What's wrong? What has happened?"

She said Ronnie had been shot and he was dead. I had planned to pick Ronnie up in a few hours. How could this be? I then spoke with Daddy. He said he left Ronnie's apartment and been home no more than an hour when a sheriff's deputy knocked on the door, telling him he needed to go to Memorial Hospital because Ronnie had been shot. When Daddy arrived at the emergency room, he was met by his ex-wife, who said, "Ronnie is dead."

We had very little information about what had really taken place. Two witnesses were present when Ronnie was shot, the roommate and a girl Ronnie was dating, yet gave conflicting accounts as to what happened.

The roommate, the nephew of our father's ex-wife, told police Ronnie was sitting on the bed playing with the .410 shotgun when it went off, shooting him under the chin. But before the roommate called for medical assistance, he called his aunt (my dad's ex-wife). She came over and the two of them bathed Ronnie, changed his clothes— destroying crucial evidence—before calling an ambulance.

When the young girl Ronnie was dating was questioned, she said she and Ronnie were arguing, and Ronnie went upstairs and shot himself.

The lies by the roommate and girl caused what I believe was a murder with a staged death scene, to be closed as suicide with no actual investigation having been done.

Knowing something was wrong, I called the police department for the next thirty-five years, pleading for them to investigate Ronnie's death. I was always told they were looking into it and someone would get back with me, or the investigator I needed to talk with was away on vacation. Ironic as it seems, within forty-five minutes to an hour of calling law enforcement, my dad called me to say, "Leave it alone. Leave it the hell alone before you get someone else killed."

Little did I know the impact of those words.

There was tremendous corruption in Gulfport at that time. My dad was in law enforcement and, sad to say, also involved in illegal gambling. I realized later that although he knew what really happened to Ronnie, he could never tell the truth about it. He kept the secret and carried the guilt for thirty-five years, afraid for his own life and that of his surviving kids.

I didn't know any of this at the time, so I kept calling the police. When I called, they would call my dad and tell him to stop me from asking questions. My refusal to shut up about Ronnie did, in fact, lead to another death.

On November 27, 2002, I was having breakfast with my dad at Waffle House in Gulfport, when I noticed his demeanor change. His face turned blood red as he stared at someone sitting behind me. Dad mumbled the words, "Son of a bitch."

I turned around to see who Dad was looking at when he said in a hiss, "Turn back around. Don't look at that son of a bitch."

A few minutes later the SOB got up from his table and walked past us. I had no idea who he was. He glared down at me and then smirked at my father before walking out the door. When he was gone, Dad asked, "Do you know who that was?"

"No. I only know that you don't like him."

"His name is Bill Wiley." Next came the words that tore my heart out yet confirmed what I had suspected all those years. "He is the old boy who killed Ronnie."

That was the first time my father admitted Ronnie's death was a murder and not a suicide. I don't know what caused him to open up to me. Maybe it was seeing the man who had killed his son sitting just feet away from us. Or maybe he was letting me know that if anything happened to him, it wouldn't be suicide. Whatever the reason, he made the decision not to be intimidated and live in fear any longer. Little did he know those words would cost him his life.

On April 18, 2003, almost five months after he told me about Bill Wiley, my dad was gunned down in his driveway. His car was gone, his Masonic and Shriner rings and his watch were gone, and his life insurance policy had been cashed out two months before his death.

I received a call around midnight from my dad's attorney friend, asking me if I was alright. Not knowing the reason for his call, I told him I was fine. He then said, "Phyllis, you don't know what your dad did today, do you?"

Still unaware of what was going on, I thought maybe the two of them had been to a casino and my father had won a lot of money. I said, "Oh, gosh, what did Daddy do now?"

He said, "Your daddy committed suicide today."

I remember falling to the floor screaming, "No! Please God, no! Not my daddy."

He was my hero, my life.

Before leaving for Gulfport, I went to my daughter and told her and the grandkids what had happened. I remember feeling as though

I was in a dream and could not wake up. I knew my dad would not do this. He would not hurt me this way, especially knowing how I was devastated by my little brother's death.

I arrived at the Riemann Funeral Home in Gulfport around 6:30 the next morning, where I was met by coroner Gary Hargrove. He came across to me as very cold and uncaring. He said my father had committed suicide by shooting himself in the head with his service revolver. He stated that a woman, who had been living with my dad as a housekeeper for the past month, had gone to the store to get him cigarettes. When she returned, she found him dead in the driveway.

I expressed my disbelief that my dad shot himself. It was then that Hargrove became very defensive. He insisted my father shot himself, and did it because he knew he would be going to jail for writing bad checks. He also told me things Dad had recently sold that wouldn't be found in the house.

I remember thinking, how could this man, someone Dad never mentioned, know so much about what was going on in my father's life? Was I to believe he learned all that information overnight? Red flags began to appear. Gary Hargrove and the police wanted me to believe my dad, Lieutenant Dan Anderson of the Harrison County Sheriff's office for almost forty years, walked out into his driveway at 4:30 in the afternoon during rush hour traffic, and took his service revolver and shot himself in the head. They claimed there were no witnesses, even though he lived so close to the houses next door, you could sit on the porch and talk without having to raise your voice.

Further, he lived on a heavily traveled street with people either driving or walking by all day.

My father died from a single gunshot wound to the head. His death was immediately declared a suicide. From day one, I expressed my belief that Daddy had been murdered, and his case needed to be investigated. All I got in response were lame excuses from Hargrove that justified the suicide finding. I believe Hargrove lied to me from our first conversation. The judge my dad worked for as a part-time bailiff confirmed that much of what Hargrove told me was untrue.

Other things I found highly suspicious about my father's death were that his car was gone, alleged to have been sold shortly before he died, his Masonic and Shriner rings and watch were gone, never to be found, the house was stripped of most valuables, and his life insurance policy had been forged and cashed out by his attorney friend just two months before he was killed.

Yet, with all the evidence I've presented to law enforcement and the coroner, they will not change the manner of death to homicide. All my requests for an investigation have been denied. I have been refused access to the scene photos and told that the 9-1-1 call has been destroyed.

Last year, in response to my third Freedom of Information Act request, I received a form stating that the shell casings from the alleged suicide were destroyed on April 22, 2003, just four days after my dad's death. It was signed by two officers and what appeared to be my signature as the third. I questioned why they would destroy the shell casing of my dad's gun so quickly, even though I had told them right away that I didn't think his gun was used to kill him and I was sure he had been murdered. And then I realized I had not received that form in 2003. And that wasn't my signature. I was totally shocked at the extent to which the authorities had gone to cover up the truth.

Dad's autopsy showed his hair and nails were cut, he was well groomed—no signs of depression or that he neglected himself. There was no record that my father appeared depressed prior to his death, and neither had Ronnie. Although they were thirty-five years apart, the similarities between the suspicious circumstances surrounding both their deaths was stunning to me.

I believe law enforcement lied and covered up facts about Ronnie and then Daddy's death for over fifty years. They have ignored, stone-walled or denied every attempt I made to get to the truth. In both cases, there was either no investigation or an insufficient one. Each was ruled a suicide within a matter of minutes. I believe there is more than sufficient evidence to have both cases re-opened and properly investigated. These are among the questions I want answered:

Why weren't any of our family members interviewed regarding either my brother or father's deaths?

Why was evidence destroyed so quickly?

Why wasn't the girlfriend, the roommate or his aunt charged with tampering with evidence for moving and bathing Ronnie's body before notifying the authorities?

Why would law enforcement not release any information to our family on deaths that been ruled suicides?

A Gulfport police captain said he conducted recorded interviews of most of the people who I felt were implicated in Ronnie's death. However, after those interviews, he claimed that his audio machine malfunctioned and all their statements were lost. How convenient is that?

Why did coroner Gary Hargrove lie about the circumstances surrounding my father's death? My dad was going to jail for writing bad checks, and had sold or pawned everything in his house due to his gambling habit. Where was my dad's car, jewelry, and all the valuables that should have been in the house?

Dad's housekeeper had supposedly left the house to get Dad some cigarettes. Yet there were several packs found in both his bedroom and living room. I believe she was a plant to keep an eye on him. Do you find it a bit too convenient that she just happened to be absent when Dad died? If she really did go for cigarettes, there should have been a full carton in the house. There wasn't. Where were they?

Why will they not release any of the scene photos?

I have information that connects Ronnie and Daddy's murders to the murders of Pauline Pusser, wife of Buford Pusser of Walking Tall fame, and Judge Vincent Sherry and his wife Margaret in 1987. I believe all these cases are tied together and being covered up by law enforcement due to their connection to what is known as the Dixie

Mafia. The laws need to be changed to protect the victims and their families, not the criminals and corrupt law enforcement.

It is my hope that one day my story will be told in a court of law, and justice will be served. Maybe reading this will help other families in their quest for information and spare them any unnecessary pain.

I have diligently fought for justice for my brother and father, and will continue to be their voices against the coldblooded killers who took them from me. The killer(s) not only murdered them, I died inside, as well. I pray justice will come soon.

PHYLLIS ANDERSON COOK, Ron's sister

CHAPTER TEN

Jessica Starr

BY ALEXIA STARR
Jessica's sister

In March 2016, my sister Jessica died in Glendale, Arizona. I think her boyfriend Pete intentionally killed her by withholding addictive medication from her. Before I get into the details of Jessica's death, I want to begin with the history of violence between them, and how he first started taking away her pain medications to control her.

Pete was becoming more and more violent toward her, so on May 19, 2015, Jessica booked tickets for her and her two children to fly home to New York. Pete found a text regarding the scheduled flight in Jessica's phone. The text was sent to Ronald, her daughter's father, asking him to pick them up at the airport.

That same day, Pete canceled the airline flight and held her and my nephew (his own son) hostage at knifepoint. He also took away her medications to make her totally dependent on him.

Jessica called 9-1-1 and the person who answered the phone asked Jessica to put her phone on speaker, which she did. The dispatcher asked Pete if he had a knife to my nephew's throat and he said, "Yes." A SWAT team responded, and Pete was taken into custody and subsequently convicted for his actions.

I'm not sure of the details, but somehow Pete went to jail for only about a month and was put on probation for two years. The judge ordered him to stay away from Jessica and the kids until the end of his probation. However, he continued living with her until the day she died. Although contrary to the court order, we later found out that the living arrangements were approved by Pete's probation officer, who apparently thought he had the authority to overturn the judge's ruling. Jessica lived in complete fear for the entire last year of her life.

We have court records, Jessica's Facebook messages to friends, and a medical report which shows that her primary care physician saw the police report of Pete being arrested for domestic violence with Jessica's medication in his pocket.

On November 7, 2015, six months after the knifepoint-hostage incident, Jessica told a Facebook friend how much more abusive Pete was becoming. The friend sent screenshots, and in one message Jessica stated, "One day I feel I won't wake up because of him."

Now I am going to tell you about Jessica's death.

First, I am going to discuss a phone call between my mother and Pete that took place immediately after Jessica died. Pete was crying, and he said, "Jess kept pushing and pushing me until I couldn't take it anymore." My mother tried to stay calm, but her voice was shaking, and she asked him what he was talking about. He said, "She was going to leave me for Ronald, and she was taking my kids from me. I had to stop her. She was going to fuck Ronald again, and I couldn't let that happen."

My mother asked him what he did to stop her, but he hung up. He called back later to explain how she died. "I was steam-cleaning the bedroom carpet and simultaneously washing blankets (he was not known for ever doing housework). While I was working, Jess sat on the bed watching TV. Then she started having an asthma attack, so I gave her the nebulizer. She said she was getting worse and then she just stopped breathing. I tried doing CPR and then I called 9-1-1."

Pete kept calling my mother back and changed his story of how Jessica died each time. For example, in one scenario he told my mother Jessica fell against the bedroom dresser and knocked everything to the floor. Later he said she leaned against the bedroom wall and knocked down all the pictures, leaving broken glass everywhere. What he did not tell my mother, my brother, the hospital, or the medical examiner, is that Jessica vomited for a long period of time before she stopped breathing. The EMS and hospital reports state that there was vomit in all four quadrants of Jessica's stomach. He did tell a family member that he was steam-cleaning vomit, but claimed it was his son's, not Jessica's.

When my mother called the hospital to ask what happened to my sister, instead of giving the phone to a doctor, they handed it to Pete. My mother hung up and called back, insisting that she speak with a doctor. Whoever answered claimed they were putting a doctor on the line, but I have a difficult time believing that my mother was actually speaking to a doctor. He was incredibly unprofessional and sounded completely uneducated. He used the word "stuff" repeatedly. He said, "We tried to give her CPR and stuff, and we gave her all kinds of medication and stuff." I understand that he probably works in an area with a lot of uneducated people who do not understand medical terminology, however, it sounded to me like he was uneducated. His communication skills were clearly lacking.

I also want to point out that when my brother first arrived in Arizona, my niece told him she saw Pete drag Jessica's unresponsive body from the bedroom to the hallway, and then close the bedroom door before calling 9-1-1. The EMS report also says they found her in the hallway, not the bedroom where Pete told everybody she died. I don't know if this is relevant, but my niece also said Pete was spoon-feeding Jessica ice cream with a baby spoon just before her death, and she vomited purple-blue stuff before passing away. Pete's statement to the medical examiner was that Jessica went into the bathroom (which is in their bedroom) and when she came back out, she leaned against the wall and collapsed. So how did she end up in the hallway?

Pete tried to have Jessica cremated within a few hours of her death without giving our family any chance to see her. He then realized that because they weren't married, he needed my mother's consent. So, he called my mother demanding that she sign my sister's body over to him. He told her to call the hospital to tell them to release the body to him, or they would throw her body away. He called day and night to the point where my mother started to get sick from the stress, which I believe was his intention. Pete knew my mother had epilepsy, and stress with a lack of sleep will trigger seizures.

My brother and I believe Pete was trying to confuse my mother into signing the body over to him. When we told her to absolutely not answer his calls anymore, Pete started calling other family members, demanding they force my mother to sign. When Pete somehow found out that my mother was fighting for an autopsy, he really got desperate and threatened all of us. Because I answered my mother's phone and wouldn't tell her when he called, he started texting me, as follows:

> Pete: Can you call these people and tell them to let me release her body, so they can fix her up and get her ready?
>
> Me: They will release her body to Frankie (Jessica's father) tonight then the funeral will be tomorrow, no?
>
> Pete: All he has to do is give the hospital; permission to let the mortuary pick up her body. We're going to schedule the funeral service for Thursday, that's enough time for Frankie and Ben (Jessica's brother) to see her.
>
> Me: They will both be there tonight.
>
> Pete: If she is not released they will lose her, we waited long enough.
>
> Me: Ben and Frankie will see her tonight and sign, do not worry. I will call the hospital now, she will be fine.
>
> Pete: You guys need to tell them I will take care of everything or else she will get lost. They need to take her body and get her ready asap.

His last text made no sense, because there was nothing to get her body ready for—he was planning a fifteen-minute viewing and a cremation. The funeral service he was talking about was just his family getting together in a place with photos and flowers to talk about Jessica. That is a memorial service, not a funeral service. He was planning to have her cremated days before that particular event.

We aren't the only ones who thought Pete had something to do with Jessica's death. Right after she died, her friends began messaging my mother saying they felt Pete was responsible. They sent a number of screenshots of messages and text conversations they had with Jessica about Pete's abuse.

Although an autopsy was performed, much of the report is based on Pete's statements. The medical examiner listed information about Jessica's heart, lungs, etc., and then wrote a one-paragraph summary of why he concluded her death to be an accident. Pete is mentioned over and over in that brief summary.

The report suggests that Jessica accidentally overdosed on pain medication. But pain medications cause constricted pupils, and the EMS report says her pupils were dilated, consistent with withdrawal. Further, the medication listed on the toxicology report did not reach a toxic level.

Pete also told Jessica's friend, who recorded the conversation, that Jessica could not have overtaken the medications, because he had them in his pocket, as always.

The medical examiner also failed to note that Jessica had vomited violently before dying. In fact, he didn't report vomiting at all. He also missed a small scar on her lung and that she had a fatty liver.

The medical examiner initially refused the autopsy saying there was no reason not to believe the information Pete provided, and felt it to be a waste of time and resources. The organ donor foundation insisted on an autopsy, so he finally agreed. However, I think he missed far too many things to be considered human error.

I also think the medical examiner listed only the medication Pete had in his pocket. Too many of her medication were missing from the toxicology report, some of which should have shown up for months after the last dose was taken. I have possession of documents that list Jessica's medication from the pharmacy. These are the medications Jessica was on every day:

- Oxycodone 15 mg every 4 hours
- Tizanidine 4 mg every 8 hours
- Diazepam 10 mg twice a day
- Zolpidem 10 mg once a day
- Promethazine 12.5 mg once a day

Only oxycodone was listed on the toxicology report, and it hadn't reached a toxicity level.

I thought toxicology tested only for opiates, benzodiazepines and street drugs, but the autopsy report shows the oxycodone, Benadryl, and Tylenol (none at toxicity levels), and a nausea medication that did not have a level at all. So why list it? Further, even if Pete withheld her medication for an entire week, diazepam should still have shown on the toxicology report. When looking at a particular drug's toxicity level, we must also consider a person's tolerance to it. For example, while the oxycodone level on my sister's toxicity report was not considered toxic, because I weigh 103 pounds and have never taken oxycodone, that amount might be enough to kill me. Jessica weighed close to 200 pounds, so her tolerance would be very strong, especially since it was without all the other daily medications.

One final point is that we did try to file police reports. My brother and Jessica's father tried, but there's no police station in Glendale, Arizona. Those in the surrounding areas said they had no jurisdiction, and refused to take a report. When Ronald arrived, he also attempted to file a report, but they wouldn't accept anything from him either. He actually spoke to Jessica a day before she died, we have a screenshot of the call record. She told him that Pete was planning to kill her, but Ronald thought she was just paranoid.

I haven't sent the evidence to authorities as of yet. However, I did make a YouTube video with all the information, and it quickly began to get many views, shares and comments. When Pete found out about the video, he had a friend contact my mother saying he died of liver complications. The friend sent my mother screenshots of a group conversation where Pete's brother tells the group about his passing, and instructs the group not to tell anyone or post it on Facebook, as the family did not want anyone to find out. However, the brother posted it publicly a few days later.

Our fight to get justice for Jessica is not over. On the contrary, it has only just begun.

ALEXIA STARR, Jessica's sister

CHAPTER ELEVEN

Daniel Ray Underwood

BY DONNA UNDERWOOD
Daniel's mom

My son Daniel was thirty-three when he died from a gunshot wound to the head on September 4, 2008, during an altercation with Rebecca, his girlfriend, in his home in Sulphur Springs, Texas. She had been living there a short time, having moved in on the weekend of July 4.

Earlier that evening, Daniel and Rebecca, along with friends Robin and Maria, had been to several bars. Maria then accompanied Daniel and Rebecca back to Daniel's house. According to Maria, Daniel and Rebecca got into a heated argument when Daniel confronted Rebecca and accused her of taking a large sum of cash he discovered missing. His online bank account had also been logged into.

Visibly upset, Daniel demanded answers from Rebecca about the whereabouts of his money. Maria sensed the tension and went into a bedroom, but could hear a full-blown argument continuing.

After hearing Rebecca call her name, Maria exited the bedroom. Standing only a few feet away from her in the hallway, Daniel and Rebecca had a 12-gauge shotgun between them. Maria said the following moments were a blur. There was shouting, a struggle over the gun, and then a deafening shotgun blast which hit Daniel in the face, mortally wounding him. Maria began to look for a phone to call 9-1-1, but Rebecca ordered her not to, saying "Not yet." Eventually Rebecca called 9-1-1.

I obtained a copy of that conversation. She began by stating, "My fiancée just shot himself in the head by accident!" She then went into a fit of screaming and crying but was able to clearly answer questions from the dispatcher. She then repeated her initial statement (shot by accident) before reverting back to hysterics.

Upon their arrival, law enforcement immediately began taking photos of Daniel in the hallway (he presumably still had a pulse) and assessing the scene before allowing emergency responders access into the house to begin treating Daniel. The crime scene was processed very quickly and lots of key evidence was not collected from the house, including Rebecca's bloody clothes. Interestingly, though, test results showed elevated amounts of gunshot residue particles on Rebecca, which could be fairly significant, considering Daniel had zero amounts on his right hand.

Even before Daniel took his last breath, Rebecca considered everything he owned to be hers. While Daniel was dying on the hall floor, she called several people from his cellphone, claiming to be his beneficiary.

Our family was not allowed to enter Daniel's home. Instead, police instructed us to go to the hospital. Daniel was already in the ambulance and ready for transport. Once there, we were not allowed to see him—not even briefly. Unbeknownst to us until later, there was a small group of people at the hospital who were listening for news about Daniel's condition, then reporting it to Rebecca. She learned of Daniel's passing at virtually the same time as the family.

Some of those who were relaying private details about Daniel's medical condition to Rebecca would later try to clean the crime scene before we were even notified that the house had been released by the police. Rebecca's brother portrayed himself as an officer of the law, and said the law required us to have a biohazard team come in to clean before we would be allowed to enter the home.

Several hours later, Rebecca arrived at the police department for her interview, and brought along her ex-boyfriend, whom she wanted to get back together with. Rebecca was known to have run around with other men even when she was living with Daniel. And his death in no way slowed her down in that regard.

I obtained the recording of Rebecca's police interview and made the following observations.

Upon entering the interrogation room and prior to questioning, Rebecca asked if she could have Daniel's wallet and credit cards, which were in his name only. When questioning began, Rebecca attempted to portray an idyllic relationship—one with no arguments or financial issues. She also stated that a large amount of Daniel's cash was missing.

Daniel had left his job recently to pursue one with a better schedule for him to spend more time with his children, and had cashed out his 401K, which was around twenty-five-thousand dollars. In less than a month, there was no money left. While referencing the missing cash, Rebecca held up her hand to admire a ring on her finger (it was Daniel's ex-wife's ring) and laughed, claiming she thinks that the missing money was used to purchase her a bigger ring, because he had always said five karats wasn't big enough for her.

Rebecca had a recoil bruise from the butt of the gun on her thigh area that she mentioned to the detective during her interview. Yet she posted a comment online years later contradicting herself, claiming the bruise was from them making love. During the interview, she reminded the detective that she had given him tips on other cases. He acknowledged that he had talked to her before. Rebecca continually referred to the lead detective, as "my good friend, Bo," as she smiled and made quotation marks in the air with her fingers to emphasize her statement. The acknowledgment that Rebecca had prior dealings with the detective could account for why I believe she was treated with kid gloves during the interview which, in my opinion, didn't follow appropriate protocols and lacked professionalism.

Police did not question the conflicting versions of Rebecca's story, although she continually contradicted herself. She agreed to take a polygraph test about the facts of that evening but backed out after consulting with her attorney. However, she told numerous people that she did take the test and passed it with flying colors.

Our family was assured there would not be any bias shown during Daniel's death investigation, but after reviewing the taped interviews, we were astonished to witness not only the appearance of bias, but that it was a reality.

After the interview, Rebecca rushed back to Daniel's house with her friends and began gathering up everything she could steal of his personal belongings to sell for cash, including his favorite pool cues, jewelry, tools, laptop, and phone. Rebecca then deleted information from his laptop and cell phone.

Later the same day, I called Rebecca and requested that Daniel's cellphone and Dodge Durango truck be returned. Rebecca seemed to be in disbelief that the family expected to obtain his belongings. We were totally unprepared for the way Rebecca screamed and cursed at us. Rebecca felt that as Daniel's fiancée, she was his beneficiary and entitled to everything he owned, including his home. Oddly, she was the only person who ever said she and Daniel were engaged.

Contrary to the hunky-dory relationship Rebecca described to the police, friends and family were aware that all was not well with them. Rebecca had mentioned to several people that she was still in love with another man, was tired of Daniel and planning to leave him. At the same time, Daniel told several friends that his future plans did not include her, and she was his soon-to-be ex, but had to tread carefully due to her violent nature.

Daniel's death was almost immediately ruled a suicide—before any forensic testing and even prior to questions being asked of the people who were around him that night. Those people could have told of the arguments and tension that had been escalating between Daniel and Rebecca prior to the shooting. As far as the investigators talking with anyone who might have had pertinent information, it seemed that was entirely irrelevant to them, and never occurred.

The crime scene was processed quickly without using standard procedures. There is certain protocol that should be followed during death investigations, even those presumed to be suicide. At the very least, Daniel's death should have been treated as a basic death investigation, which could have turned out to be a homicide. As a professional law enforcement officer, the investigator cannot assume anything. Ensuring the integrity of the evidence by establishing and maintaining a chain of custody is vital to any investigation. The gunshot residue collection kits that were used that night have long been obsolete, according to the Trace Evidence Lab in Dallas, even for a small town such as Sulphur Springs. Neither the gun nor shell were dusted for fingerprints. The entire house was in disarray. There was obviously some kind of struggle in the living room, yet police didn't deem it important enough to photograph. Boxes were packed and taped up with only her belongings in them.

At the time of Daniel's death, Maria was traumatized—she had just witnessed the violent death of a dear friend. Rebecca insisted Maria tell authorities that Daniel had shot himself. She also knew (as many locals did) that Rebecca was likely an informant for the Sulphur Springs Police Department, and liked to brag about having such good friends within the police department. Maria was terrified for her own safety and that of her small children. So, when she was interviewed by the police the night of Daniel's death, she stated what she was told to say by Rebecca.

Maria was again contacted by authorities a short time later, and, although she was sick and scheduled for surgery the next day, she tried to recant her previous statement. She admitted that Daniel did not shoot himself, and said she had witnessed Rebecca pull the trigger. However, she was treated with a hostile attitude from them. They refused to consider any other possibility. Daniel's death had been ruled a suicide, and that was end of the story as far as they were concerned.

Over the years, more and more people have come forward with new information from that night. Rebecca has actually confessed to several people who have contacted the family, including a former neighbor, in 2012. Not being from the area, the former neighbor figured Rebecca was just a local dopehead talking a big game. That is, until she read an article posted on Facebook about Daniel's death and saw Rebecca's name. She reached out to the Underwood family and informed us of what she had been told. While it was difficult to hear, we are very grateful for her willingness to tell what she knows. Both she and Maria are available and willing to discuss Daniel's case with the authorities.

Daniel's death was violent, tragic and senseless. After obtaining all the case files, along with the autopsy report, photos and lab results showing traces of gunshot residue on the person of interest, and zero amounts on Daniel's right hand that allegedly held the gun when it fired, we strongly believe his death was not a suicide. The family is seeking for the cause of death on Daniel's death certificate to be officially changed from suicide to homicide or undetermined. That would make it possible for Daniel's case to be re-opened. Then, the investigation needs to be turned over to an outside agency with which the investigators have no personal relationship with Rebecca, or anyone else involved with the case.

Daniel was a good person. A loving son, brother and a devoted father. His case deserves a proper investigation.

DONNA UNDERWOOD, Daniel's mom

CHAPTER TWELVE

Jack L. Robinson

BY TAMMY SCOTT DOWNS
Jack's daughter

This story is about the murder of my father and the nightmare it created for me and my family. It forever affected the way I look at life, and opened my eyes to the good and bad in the world.

Prior to that fateful day in 1996, I lived my life like most people. I went to work, shopped and went to baseball games—never anticipating that one day I'd get that terrible phone call that would take my breath away and cause my knees to buckle. It was a call I don't wish on anybody. It is a pain that never goes away.

My father was born and raised in the Olympia Mills Village area of South Carolina. He joined the Air Force and made a career of it. After retiring, he worked as a civilian employee at Moncreif Army Hospital at Fort Jackson, and retired from there, as well.

While in the Air Force, we lived in Cheyenne, Wyoming, Rapid City, South Dakota, and Bermuda. He loved his family and we had some great times but eventually he and my mother divorced. He remarried about five years later and divorced fifteen years after that.

My dad and two aunts came to visit me in Florida. He loved the beach and enjoyed playing at the beach with my sons. He made sure my boys had a chance to take a train ride from Florida to Columbia, South Carolina, and then he gave me a big train set to put around our Christmas tree. He helped feed the homeless and other people in need. My father had a good heart and would give you the shirt off his back. He was a good man.

On Saturday, August 17, 1996, at around 6 p.m., my father was murdered. At the time, I was visiting my mother, and my sons were with their dad for the weekend. I was notified the next morning by family. This was the phone call that changed our lives forever.

"You need to come home to Columbia, because your father was murdered."

As soon as I heard those words, my mother packed a bag, and off to my house I went to pack a few things and then pick my sons up at their father's. My emotions were going wild; the questions running through my head seemed endless. I couldn't keep up with them.

We arrived at my aunt's home that Sunday. On Monday, I had to identify my father's body and speak with detectives at the Richland County Sheriff's Office.

According to them, at about 6 p.m. my father had gone to the Rosewood Boat Landing, today known as the Jordan Memorial Boat Ramp, located in his old neighborhood in Olympia. They had no clue as to why he went there. Three eyewitnesses told detectives they saw my father and another man talking and assumed they were acquainted. The two then walked into a nearby clearing where they talked. One witness claimed my father said, "What do you want? Do you want money?" The conversation became physical when the man stabbed my father in his upper body. The witnesses described the suspect as a hispanic male with an olive complexion, between twenty-five and thirty-five years old, five-foot five-inches tall and 150 to 180 pounds, with black hair and mustache.

My father was transported to the Palmetto Health Richland Hospital where, after unsuccessful surgery, he was pronounced dead.

The detectives speculated that my father could have been accosted by a stranger in a robbery attempt. They then had another theory that our family was not prepared for—they thought my father was gay and could have been murdered by his lover. Needless to say, this was totally out of left field and unacceptable to all of us.

There was no progress in solving my father's murder for eighteen months. And then a nineteen-year-old man named Max was arrested in Columbia, for brutally murdering a young woman and her three-year-old niece with a knife. He put their bodies in the trunk of his car and took them to the Congaree River, where he threw the woman's body into the woods and the little girl's body into the river.

When the police brought the suspect in for questioning about the murders, he allegedly made comments about the composite drawing of my father's killer that was on the detective's desk. Because those murders and my father's murder were committed with a knife, and the suspect's comments about the composite of my father's killer, he was also charged in Dad's death. Since the case for murdering the woman and child case was far stronger, they had all the evidence necessary to put Max in prison for life. He was charged, convicted, and sentenced to life in prison without the possibility of parole.

For my dad's case, no knife or DNA were found, so there was not enough evidence to go to court. Three years later, the suspect's charges in my father's case were dropped. The authorities neglected to inform me, or any family, of this decision.

When I discovered the case was open again, I wrote a letter to the sheriff asking what was going on with the investigation. The sheriff's office, the prosecutor, and the solicitor's office could not answer any of my questions and I was referred to the cold case division. That's when I met the new detective assigned to my dad's case.

Since then I have worked with two new detectives and the chief. We've gone through ups and downs and had our share of spats because I didn't always believe what they told me. I feared they might again wrongfully charge another man just to say they solved the case.

However, I believe progress in our relationship has been made, and I am now kept in the loop as much as possible. We get along a lot better, and I had to realize I need them and they need me.

In August 2017, I was allowed to meet with members of the news media at the Rosewood Boat Landing to discuss Dad's case. I was also able to talk about it in "Grief Diaries: Project Cold Case," a book featuring stories of unsolved homicides. The chief has also spoken to Project Cold Case several times.

While I was in Columbia, the chief told me about their efforts. They put up posters targeting the LGBT community in which my father was described as a closeted homosexual male. They claimed my father frequently visited gay bars in the Columbia area using an alias.

The detectives were also interested in a murder from January 1997, in which a sergeant from Fort Jackson was stabbed to death by a twenty-three-year-old hispanic male. The sergeant was married and had a family, yet supposedly lived a secret life as a gay man. He reportedly had anger issues and would rape and kill his victims. Apparently in this case, the victim was able to get the knife away from the sergeant and stab him to death.

Could that sergeant have had something to do with my father's murder? I guess it is possible, but the dead sergeant had no known link to my father. And I'm still not totally convinced my father was gay.

This whole thing has taken a heavy toll on me and my sons, who were close to their grandfather. Over the years, most of my family has passed away. Three of my father's siblings are gone and my surviving aunt is fragile. We no longer talk about the murder. I just found out that my cousin, who used to pal around with my father, died in July.

One fairly new development has me somewhat excited, though. Up to this point, only Dad's DNA has shown up in various tests. But in June, the detectives decided to try a new technology called M-Vac to look for DNA that may not have been previously detected. Twenty people in the group were tested, including the deceased sergeant from Fort Jackson. Hopefully this test will find something to help identify my dad's killer. As of now, I am anxiously awaiting the results. I have mixed emotions about this, because if the sergeant's DNA shows up, then we're at a dead end. But, an answer is an answer, even if it can't be pursued any further.

In closing, I want to reiterate my personal beliefs. I was raised to be in church every Sunday and Wednesday. I was baptized and believe in Jesus. I hold my beliefs close to my heart. I have always believed that marriage is to take place between a man and woman. When my father was murdered, I was in my early thirties, headstrong, and tended to speak my mind. Sometimes that got me into trouble.

When I had to sit at the big table across from all the detectives, it was one thing to hear that my father was murdered. It was another to hear that he was gay and killed by his homosexual lover. That was not the man I knew and loved. No way! My father was a church-going man who read his bible every day at the table while having breakfast, and in the evening before bed. So, this cannot be. Over the years, I thought it would get easier to accept this gay issue. It hasn't. I was even denied a spot on a radio show because of my refusal to acknowledge that those allegations might be true.

I and all the others who have shared their stories in this book are seeking the same thing—justice. We need the person(s) responsible for the death of our loved one to be held accountable. We need answers. I need truth, and proof.

We all need to be able to talk about our loved one and the good times we shared with them. We need the peace of knowing we fought so hard for them that it became exhausting. And even so, we would do it all over again.

I love you Dad, with all my heart. On August 17, you will have been gone for twenty-two years. It is time for the truth to come out and justice to be served. I am ready.

TAMMY SCOTT DOWNS, Jack's daughter

The police must obey the law
while enforcing the law.

-EARL WARREN

CHAPTER THIRTEEN

Michael S. Sanchez

BY LISA SANCHEZ-LUCERO
Michael's aunt

On June 18, 2013, my twenty-seven-year-old nephew Michael was brutally murdered in Albuquerque, New Mexico.

In early April of that year, Michael called his brother Isaac to tell him that he was having trouble with his neighbors and their dogs. He said the dogs were getting under his home at night and keeping him awake. He also said the dogs would wait for him to exit his home in the morning and then chase after him, nipping at his ankles. He stated he had already been bitten on two different occasions.

Michael said he had been to the neighbor's house to complain, but nothing had been done to keep the dogs properly fenced in, so they wouldn't be running loose in the neighborhood. Isaac told him not to fight with the neighbors, but to call Animal Control and file a formal complaint. On April 12, Michael made his first call to Animal Control, according to the report he filed that day. The report stated there were aggressive dogs in the neighborhood that were habitually loose.

Papers show that on April 13, Animal Control responded to the call and educated dog owner Ricardo Villanueva Cordova on the leash law, and the animal at large and animal licensing laws. They issued a verbal warning for the leash law, and a citation for the animal licensing law. Cordova was given a date as to when he had to be in compliance with the warning and citation issued to him that day, or additional charges would be filed.

On April 25, Michael made his second call to Animal Control. He again stated that aggressive dogs were habitually loose in the neighborhood. He informed Animal Control that he had already talked with the neighbor but said the neighbor's response was, "He didn't like the dogs and he didn't want them."

On that same day, Animal Control again responded. They re-contacted Cordova and explained that if he didn't want the dogs he could surrender them, but otherwise he had to comply with the laws. They gave him until May 17, to surrender the animals or get into compliance. Cordova said he understood that failure to comply would result in a criminal complaint.

Then on June 18, the morning of the murder, Michael was upset. He had received a promotion and raise on his job to be effective that day, but he hadn't slept due to Cordova's dogs still being loose and under his home making noise the previous night. According to neighbors who witnessed the confrontation that morning, Michael went to Cordova's residence and explained that the dogs had again kept him awake all night and that he was going to call Animal Control again. Cordova threatened Michael, telling him to, "Come over here, I've got something for you." Michael ignored him, returned to his vehicle and left for work.

Michael stopped for gas at the Valero station at the intersection of 141 98th Street NW, and Central Avenue at 8:10 a.m. According to security footage and eyewitness statements, Michael approached the cashier, paid for his gas, and returned to his vehicle. As he began to pump gas, Cordova sped into the gas station and came to an abrupt stop behind Michael. Michael saw him and began to walk toward him.

Cordova approached Michael very fast, and immediately stabbed him in the stomach. Michael turned to run, lost his footing and fell to the ground. Cordova pursued him and began stabbing Michael in the back. Somehow in the struggle, Michael was able to turn around. Cordova applied his knee to Michael's chest and continued to slash and stab as Michael screamed for help. Cordova is six-foot two-inches tall and 220 pounds, while Michael was five-foot three-inches and 150 pounds. Cordova finally stopped his attack when a UPS driver ran toward him. At that point, Cordova ran to his vehicle. The UPS driver and several other witnesses called 9-1-1. Michael got up, stumbled to his vehicle, and collapsed.

First responders worked feverishly on Michael, resuscitating him and then transporting him to the hospital, where he was rushed into surgery. They removed part of his lung, but there were just too many injuries to his internal organs. According to the autopsy report, all together there were twenty-nine stab wounds with multiple wounds to the chest, back, abdomen, right groin and hip, heart, lungs, liver and several defensive lacerations on his hands and arms. Despite aggressive treatment Michael continued to bleed extensively, and died on the operating table at 10:45 a.m.

Back at the gas station, the police were on the scene. They were informed by witnesses of Cordova's description and license plate number. The plate number produced the killer's address and the police were at his residence within minutes of the attack.

Upon their arrival, they encountered Cordova's sister Rosa and their mother, Socorro Cordova. Rosa told the authorities that her brother was not home, and was probably on his way to Mexico.

Cordova's long-time girlfriend Ofelia then showed up. She told the police that Cordova had called her. He told her he had just killed his neighbor, the police were after him, and he'd be going to jail. He told her to go be with his mother. She also stated that Cordova was on his way to Mexico.

How is it that both Rosa and Ofelia were able to tell authorities within minutes of the murder that Cordova was on his way to Mexico? Had the two women already talked on the phone, and agreed to tell police that the murderer was headed for Mexico?

Personally, I think Ofelia was sent to his sister's home in an attempt to create a diversion. I think Cordova met his father at Ofelia's home and exchanged vehicles. Then he disappeared, supposedly never speaking with or seeing any of his family ever again. A police search of Rosa's home and the neighborhood failed to produce any evidence.

In my opinion, that was the full extent of the police investigation. Once Cordova's family put them on the trail to Mexico, they no longer continued to search for him in Albuquerque or the surrounding areas. This was just the beginning of our frustration with the authorities.

Immediately after Michael's funeral, my husband Carlos and I began calling the detective in charge of Michael's case, whom I'll call Detective Smith. It took several attempts before he returned our calls. When we finally talked with him, he said he was busy working on the case. We stopped calling in order to let him do his job. After a month or so, Carlos began calling him again and left several messages. When the detective finally called back, he sounded irritated, and wanted to know why my husband was calling when he was not Michael's real father. My husband explained that Michael's biological father did not raise Michael, nor did he ever pay child support to my sister.

My sister divorced Richard, Michael's father, when she was eight months pregnant with Michael. Richard never knew his son, nor was he ever active in Michael's life. When my sister became ill and passed away in 2001, she left my husband and myself as guardians of Michael, so he would become our son. We are the ones who finished raising him. He remained in our home until he was twenty-three years old.

We put him through school, went to all his activities, helped him buy his first home, and gave him all the love he needed.

Michael's natural father didn't want our family to come to the forefront because he planned to sue Animal Control, the Valero gas station where Michael was murdered, and the mobile home park where Michael lived. He held fundraisers, claiming he needed burial expenses for his son. Then he sold all Michael's personal belongings—home, car, gun, everything he could get his hands on. Our explanation to the detective did absolutely no good. He ended the call stating, "Michael has a living biological father, and that is who I will be answering to."

I truly believe the reason why the detective only wanted to deal with Richard, Michael's father, was because Michael's father never called him. Thanks to Richard and the detective, we were shut out of the investigation from the very beginning. But that didn't stop me from conducting my own investigation.

With the help of a friend who was a private investigator, a friend who worked at the Department of Motor Vehicles, and a friend who worked in law enforcement, we began gathering personal information about Cordova and his family. He comes from a large family that included both parents, five brothers, three sisters, many nieces and nephews, and his long-time girlfriend and her two children.

His family is originally from Durango, Mexico, where Richard is known as Sasquatch because of his physical size. We learned the addresses where he and all his family were living, the cars they drove, and where they all worked. We began staking out their homes to see their comings and goings. And we began following them to see where they were going. Carefully keeping notes on everything, we parked outside their homes for all the holidays, hoping to see Cordova show up for Mother's Day or Father's Day.

I finally realized we were way over our heads, and didn't have the resources needed to continue our efforts. After all, we were dealing with dangerous people who helped cover up for the murderer. I also realized it wasn't fair to my other children or to my mother, missing holidays with our own family because of trying to conduct our own investigation.

I finally faxed a three-page letter to the authorities containing the information we had gathered, because I was tired of them not doing their job, and hoped they would act on the information I provided. In the meantime, we continue our fight for justice by putting wanted posters on Facebook, Twitter and Instagram. We organized a group to help distribute and put up posters throughout our city.

We've been successful getting Crime Stoppers to post Cordova on their website and Facebook page, and they offered a one-thousand-dollar reward. We were successful getting America's Most Wanted to feature Cordova on their website and Facebook pages. We also got Unsolved Mysteries to feature his picture on their website and Facebook pages. In addition, Fugitive Watch put out an all-points bulletin for Cordova, and featured him on their website and Facebook pages. Victims News Online featured Michael's story in two articles.

Randall Sands, FBI forensic artist, produced twenty different progressive composites of Cordova. Michael's story is now available in the anthology, "Grief Diaries: Project Cold Case," a book featuring twenty-two families who've lost a loved one to homicide.

We've accomplished all this without help or cooperation from Michael's father or the authorities. I've been fortunate enough to have a person who recently volunteered to help. Through him, I learned Michael's case has sat cold all these years because nobody cared enough to call and demand justice for him.

We've been told that a provisional warrant has to be issued before the U.S. Marshals can go look for Cordova in Mexico. We've also been told the attorney general's office is responsible for issuing provisional warrants, which can take anywhere from one to three years. It's been five years since Michael was murdered, and this has yet to be done.

In his latest media interview, Richard plays the grieving father, but what has he done to get justice for his son? Why hasn't he stayed on top of the authorities and their investigation? Why hasn't he demanded the attorney general's office issue the provisional warrant?

Our mission for justice must continue. We must fight every day for Michael, because no one else is. I must start calling the attorney general's office demanding to know why the ball stopped there. I'm just hoping and praying they won't play the biological father card on me. It's time for the authorities to take responsibility for what they are not doing about this case, and explain their actions to our family. Michael did not deserve to die like this, and his death deserves justice.

After losing a loved one to homicide, you have so many raw emotions going on inside you, and you feel like you're dying too, but you don't die. You live through it, and that is even worse.

LISA SANCHEZ-LUCERO, Michael's aunt

Albuquerque Metro Crime Stoppers is offering a $1,000 cash reward for tips or information that lead to the capture and arrest of Ricardo Villanueva Cordova, and you may remain anonymous.

Call Crime Stoppers at (505) 843 STOP, or (505) 242 COPS.

The Michael S. Sánchez Reward Fund is currently at $2,000 and will be awarded by the Sanchez/Lucero family, for information that leads to Cordova's capture and arrest.

Without strong watchdog institutions,
impunity becomes the very foundation
upon which systems of corruption are built.

-RIGOBERTA MENCHÚ
Nobel Prize laureate

CHAPTER FOURTEEN

Brenda J. Lacombe

BY LACEY KEARNS
Brenda's niece

Imagine going to visit your grandma two days before Mother's Day, leaving shortly after midnight, and never seen alive again. Most people couldn't fathom spending an evening at their grandma's playing card games and Yahtzee and then leaving, only to disappear into thin air,  and then turn up brutally murdered. However, Aunt Brenda, and the people who held her closest to their hearts, were faced with this very nightmare.

Around 12:45 a.m. on May 16, 1982, nineteen-year-old Brenda left her grandmother's home in Lowell, Massachusetts, and vanished. On June 4, her naked, beaten and decomposing body was discovered behind a stone wall in a wooded area off Interstate-495 in nearby Harvard.

What happened within the weeks between her disappearance and the discovery of her gruesome, mangled remains has been a mystery for more than thirty-six years.

Brenda has been described by those who knew her as an outgoing young woman who kept her family and friends close. A bit of a spitfire, she always advocated for herself in situations where she knew it was warranted. She was funny, compassionate, and full of life. She loved her nine-month-old son Mathew more than anything.

It's almost ironic that Brenda holds some of my earliest childhood memories, since I personally was never granted the opportunity to meet her. I recall my mother, Brenda's older sister, taking me to the library as a child and looking at old newspaper clippings on the slide projector. These trips, of course, took place years after Brenda's body had been discovered off that quiet country road in Harvard.

My mother did her best to shield me from the emotional turmoil caused by Brenda's murder, yet I realized very early on how much it truly drained her. Maybe my perceptions of my mother's struggles are ultimately part of what caused me to want to dig deeper into the circumstances surrounding my aunt's death. As I grew older, I began threading together pieces of Brenda's case, searching for answers that are long overdue—and deserved.

However, as I began to slowly assemble pieces of the puzzle, I was totally unprepared for the surprise and frustration that came with the convoluted nature of the case.

Brenda's case began the moment she stepped outside her grand-mother's house at 735 Broadway Street at 12:45 a.m. one Sunday night in May 1982. The investigation surrounding her circumstances started initially as a missing person's report, given that her whereabouts after leaving and the state of her existence became unknown.

Brenda's grandmother thought she may have been heading over to visit an ex-boyfriend who lived on Clare Street. Most of the family who lived in his house were well known to the Lowell police, as many of them had run-ins with the law. I even heard his father was deeply connected with the notorious biker gang. He was supposedly in prison when Brenda disappeared, though.

Around 3 a.m. on Sunday, May 16, someone pounded on the door of my grandfather's home on Fulton Street in Lowell, furiously yelling for Brenda to come out of the house. They even pounded on the back door and windows. My grandfather just knew it was "the big guy up the street," Ed Davis. The son of a retired Lowell police officer, Davis stands about six-feet six-inches tall. Like many other police officers, he followed in his father's footsteps and joined the Lowell Police Department. Maybe my grandfather thought this was him because of the time he recalled Brenda getting into a car, a Trans Am, that was in front of their house, and Davis came over banging on the roof of the car, yelling for Brenda to get out of the car. The family knew back then that there was a cop living on the same street that had been harassing her, too. This all changed on June 4, when Brenda's then-unidentified body was found.

At the time, another missing person case was receiving most of the public attention—the high-profile 1981 case of Joni Webster. It was thought that Brenda's remains may have been Joni. They were similar in appearance and near the same age. So, it was reasonable to believe the body could have belonged to either Joni or Brenda.

When Brenda's sister, Bev, noticed an article in the local paper announcing discovery of the remains, Bev became suspicious that the body was Brenda. She called the police right away and explained how Brenda had vanished a few weeks prior, and the body fit Brenda's profile. She told them about Brenda's missing front tooth, courtesy of her former boyfriend, whom I'll call G.F.

Due to the gruesome nature of the partially decomposed body, authorities had to identify Brenda via dental records. The state pathologist was unable to determine the exact time of death, but noted that Brenda had possibly been deceased for weeks.

The official investigation report stated pieces of Brenda's torn clothing were strewn about her partially naked body. It was also noted that animals likely dragged part of her body through the woods, seeing that police discovered that her torso was pulled apart from her lower extremities. One detective candidly admitted to my family, "Brenda was absolutely without a doubt brutally beaten to death."

Compared to Joni Webster, Brenda's case was insignificant. My family and I have always felt that Brenda took a back seat. After her remains were identified, she vanished again back into the shadows beneath mountains of deskwork and file cabinet papers.

Even so, some investigation was done. Once word got out that the body was in fact Brenda, G.F. took off to California. This could have been due to his upcoming court case that had been postponed from April until July 1982.

One of the Lowell police officers working on the case went to California to question G.F. Instead of questioning him, however, G.F. was read his rights. This screwed up any chance of getting G.F. to talk if he did have something to do with Brenda's homicide. According to one retired Lowell homicide detective, the report documenting the trip to California was never filed because the investigation had been botched. Brenda's case seemed to be second fiddle, yet it wasn't completely ignored.

Sometime before Brenda disappeared, she and her friend Terry Gravina were called upon as state witnesses to testify in a local arson trial. Both girls feared testifying, and bench warrants were necessary to compel their appearance.

Apparently, Brenda's fright became pervasive throughout her daily life, however, and she began taking precautions before leaving her home. She often left her residence only in the company of her young son, as if the sight of a mother with her child might thwart any violence. Moreover, her efforts to keep her son at arms-length could have also been due to the fact that she truly feared for the lives of both herself and her child.

Coincidentally, it was said that Brenda may have been aware of who was purportedly behind the second fire on West Third Street in

Lowell. Not much information is known about this fire except that the building was allegedly a prostitution and drug house. The fact that most of the individuals identified in the incident were young females with prior arrest records for streetwalking might corroborate this theory. However, all that remains in this instance is a lingering suspicion in regard to Brenda's death. Maybe, unbeknownst to her, she truly had been just unfortunate enough to be loosely acquainted with some questionable individuals who later may have played a part in her demise.

Interestingly, in relation to the string of fires that happened after Brenda's disappearance, my own mother began taking care of Brenda's son. At this point, my mother strangely began receiving threatening, anonymous phone calls. The suspected male on the other end made menacing statements, such as, "Let it go or the same could happen to you and the kid."

My mother always wondered how this person knew that Brenda's son was in her care, or how they got her number in the first place. Times were different back then, and accessing this information wasn't as easy as it is nowadays. Considering my mother was married at the time, the caller would have had no way of knowing these things unless he was actively searching out these informational pieces.

To this day, compounded with the brutal murder of her sister, my mother is haunted by these phone calls, and can't help but wonder whether they were connected to the fire Brenda was to testify about in April 1982.

It is noteworthy that on April 4, 1981, at around 6 a.m., a three-alarm blaze destroyed an apartment building on 94 First Street in Lowell. According to official police reports, the fire originated in a third-floor apartment occupied by Edward Maguire and Robert Potter. The blaze spread rapidly throughout the top floor and then ignited the two bottom levels. Edward Maguire, Robert Potter, Terry Gravina, Karen Fanning (of Branch Street), and Walter Lamirande (of Broadway Street), fled from the third-floor apartment. The building was extensively damaged and left several residents homeless.

Of note, Brenda frequently bought pot from this location. The addresses, reputations, and interesting connections of those listed as present at the apartment that night certainly raises questions. Yet, Brenda's homicide investigation has not yielded any concrete answers, even after all this time.

In November 1982, a jury found Adrien "Guy" Laliberte guilty of arson for starting the fire on April 4, 1981. He was sentenced from seven to ten years in Walpole State Prison. A witness at the trial testified that he was waiting in Laliberte's car while Laliberte went inside to talk to his former girlfriend, Terry Gravina. Laliberte had been carrying around a gas can in his car for several days prior to the fire. I heard from a reliable source that during the trial, the witness went over to Laliberte with permission of the court officer and asked him if he had heard about Brenda. Laliberte was smiling and seemed very happy. He said something along the lines of, "...Yeah, you never know what will happen when you're on heavy dope." He kept smiling.

Terry Gravina testified that after she broke up with Laliberte and started seeing another man just prior to the fire, Laliberte threatened her repeatedly. Laliberte did not testify and called no witnesses in his own defense. To this day, Brenda herself stands as the sole evidence in the case. True to who I've heard Brenda was, she continues to advocate for herself from beyond the grave.

Whether or not Brenda was silenced to keep her from testifying in the arson case, or the rumors connected to the Joni Webster case and a possible killer of both young women are true, Brenda has found a way to continue fighting for her voice to be heard. She continues to do this through her own remains, through those who were closest to her, and even through second generations, such as myself. I believe it's important that she finally receive the justice she so deserves.

An interesting side note, according to an article in the New York Times, seven men were indicted on charges of setting 163 fires across eastern Massachusetts to protest cutbacks in police and fire protection, making it possibly the biggest arson case in U.S. history. Two of the defendants are police officers and two are fire fighters. In July 1984, the 83-count grand jury indictment said the blazes, which broke out in ten cities in a ten-month period in 1982, injured 280 firefighters, some seriously, and caused twenty-two million dollars in damages.

In 1984, three men indicted for their involvement in a suspected arson ring were accused of setting 106 additional blazes, including four major fires in Lowell in 1982. Leonard Kendall Jr. of Acton, Ray Norton Jr. of West Roxbury and Donald Stackpole of Scituate, were named in a twenty-five-count indictment that was included in their pending federal case naming them and four others in a suspected arson ring. Lieutenant Harold Waterhouse of the Lowell Arson Squad said that his department had believed since June 1982, the three had started a number of Lowell fires.

Ed Davis, "the big guy up the street," was named superintendent of the Lowell Police Department in 1994. Shortly thereafter, Brenda's case was reinvestigated. The assigned detective took her case file home but lost it, said Davis. When my family inquired about the protocol and procedure for handling something like that, Davis refused to discuss the matter, and kicked them out of his office. He told them to go to the Harvard Police Department from then, on since her body had been discovered there.

After sixteen years of Brenda's case being held in the back pocket of the Lowell Police Department, they now say they had no evidence and no reason to believe Brenda was murdered in Lowell. The case bounced back to Harvard and Worcester counties.

Currently I am testing out the law by utilizing the Freedom of Information Act. I'm trying to gather as much information as I can and am raising funds for an exhumation of Brenda's remains, as I truly believe she still holds the key to solving her own murder.

My advice for anyone searching for answers: Don't just accept the idea that nothing more can be done, investigation-wise or otherwise. Do your own investigation and remember that identifying sources of information is limited only by your own imagination.

Patterns do start to emerge and once I began seeing them myself, I started taking pro-active measures to solve my aunt's case. I am determined to find answers and fight for those who can't speak.

I truly believe that one person really can make a difference, even if it takes years.

LACEY KEARNS, Brenda's niece

CHAPTER FIFTEEN

Felicia A. Reeves

BY SUZAN BAYOREGEON
Felicia's sister

When the phone call came, my mind went blank. All I can say is that the voice on the other line was foreign to me. The words were muddled and my heart broke. "Felicia is dead," raced over and over in my brain. My forty-year-old sister was gone—dead in Elizabeth, New Jersey. How and when she died were not answered.

My hands were trembling as I dropped the phone and sat in a chair with tears pouring down my face. I wasn't sure what to do, I only knew I had to get to my mother's in North Carolina.

The hours and minutes that passed immediately afterward are a blur. I'm not sure how I got to North Carolina. I remember walking into my mother's living room and putting my arms around her. At that very moment all my anger, resentment and dysfunctional connections to her began to melt from heart and mind. She was no longer merely my mother. She was a mother who had just lost a child.

Mom and my stepdad told me how they learned of Felicia's death. Both stated that there were three separate phone calls received from different detectives. The information given about how my sister died was different each time.

Mom was extremely upset when one detective stated that Felicia had been a transient drug addict, became desperate, and took her own life. My mother made it very clear to the detective that Felicia had been clean for seven to nine months and had begun to get herself together. Mom demanded pictures to verify that the dead person was in fact Felicia. When the pictures came, it was obviously my sister. However, the picture's showed a very different story of how Felicia may have died. Felicia's face looked as though she had been beaten. Her left eye was black, and the right eye showed the beginnings of a shiner. Her nose was crooked, and she had cuts and bruises all over her body.

I volunteered to go to New Jersey to get my sister and bring her home. My mother would not agree to this and stated that she feared for my safety. It was decided to have my sister cremated and the cremains arrived in the mail a few days later. Felicia was buried with military honors in Black Mountain Veterans Cemetery.

From the very beginning, the Elizabeth Police Department would not answer our questions or concerns. Only when I flew to New Jersey several months later to retrieve my sister's personal belongings, death certificate, autopsy report, police report and toxicology report, did we begin to get any answers at all.

In her belongings, I found receipts that clearly showed Felicia had left the motel where her body was found and traveled to New York City, as well as made plans to go to Philadelphia. The autopsy left more questions, as body parts Felicia didn't have were included, and other things weren't mentioned such as her distinguishing tattoos and the major dental work she had done.

Felicia's toxicology report was negative for drugs and positive for alcohol. Felicia did not drink, as the drugs she had been addicted to caused severe ulcers that prevented her from drinking. There was one needle mark on her right arm, which also made no sense because she was not an IV drug user. It turned out that the motel she was found in had a history of drug and human trafficking, and was the site of a second death with similar circumstances.

I contacted the reporter who had done a story on the other death. It was with his help that I attained much of the information, and his assistance was of great value. However, once Felicia's case was re-opened, he would no longer return my phone calls or emails. Another person who reported on Felicia's case said he, too, was given different information from the police. The article he wrote about Felicia's death only raised additional questions.

I began to write letters to anyone and everyone I felt could help me with getting my sister's case properly investigated. In New Jersey, when police determine a death to be suicide, the case stays with police.

If determined to be a homicide, it's turned over to the prosecutor's office. North Carolina refused to get involved because Felicia died in New Jersey. If she disappeared from North Carolina and found dead in New Jersey, why couldn't North Carolina law enforcement assist with finding out what happened to Felicia in North Carolina?

Eventually, I began to get calls from Henderson County Sheriff's Office, explaining they could not do anything. I also received a phone call from New Jersey, demanding that I stop looking into the death of my sister. However, not long after this phone call I received a letter from then-New Jersey governor Christie's office, stating that he would have the case re-opened. I then made numerous calls and sent emails to several detectives in Elizabeth. I sent them Felicia's cellphone and other documents I had collected. Initially, the detectives were positive and encouraging. However, shortly after I sent those items, my calls and emails stopped being returned.

I then contacted the prosecutor's office asking about the status and results of the investigation. Again, I was not acknowledged. In the end, after waiting many months, I received an email stating that New Jersey could not give me the results, as I was not a New Jersey resident and the Freedom of Information Act did not cover my requests.

To the best of my knowledge, no one in North Carolina has been questioned in regard to my sister's disappearance. Many came forward initially to offer condolences, but when I questioned how they knew Felicia or their connection to her, they ran for the hills or were under police orders not to discuss the case with me.

I believe the circumstances leading to the disappearance and death of my sister clearly began in North Carolina. I do not believe her death involved drugs or human trafficking. I have reason to believe it was the result of something much more sinister but am unable to go into more detail at this time.

Once the legalities of the situation are finalized, I will be able to talk more freely.

SUZAN BAYOREGEON, Felicia's sister

Police officers see everything, and they experience everything, and they don't always act correctly.

-CHEO HODARI COKER

CHAPTER SIXTEEN

Diane Dalton Schofield

BY TWYLA DALTON JOHNSON
Diane's sister

This is the story of my only sister's tragically short life and her vicious murder.

We grew up in a dysfunctional home and our childhood was quite difficult. Our mother had mental health issues, and was physically and emotionally abusive to her husband, me, and Diane. Our parents divorced when I was ten and Diane was thirteen. We lived with our mother and our lives got worse.

We moved from our family home to a different side of town, and went to new schools. A year later, Diane began dating Kenneth Lee Schofield, became pregnant and married Schofield on August 7, 1969. She gave birth to her daughter, Shawna.

Kenneth suffered a severe addiction to heroin. Although I believe he truly loved Diane and Shawna, he loved heroin even more. Diane was married, a mother, and divorced by age sixteen. Not exactly a picture-perfect childhood.

After the divorce Diane struggled to get by, working as a hotel maid, grocery clerk, and in various retail stores. In 1974, she started working as a masseuse at the Den Massage Parlor in Des Moines, and her life changed drastically. She lived in a nicer home and drove nice cars. She was a happy and fun-loving young woman—beautiful and outgoing. She was always laughing and left a positive impression on those whose lives she touched.

In January 1975, Diane was arrested for illegally carrying a concealed .22 caliber pistol. She was put on probation, and one of the conditions was that she could no longer work as a masseuse. She reportedly began doing freelance masseuse work and started working at two local bars, the Totem Pole and Dave Salem's Foozin & Boozin.

Diane purportedly kept a book of clients she gave massages to on an outcall basis, including names, dates, and services rendered. The attorney who represented her on the concealed weapon charge shared that Diane told him several months prior to her arrest that she was asked to be an informant regarding illegal drugs, but was not specific as to who approached her. The attorney said he advised her not to do it, and doesn't believe she became an informant.

Lieutenant Dick Lamb, head of the Metropolitan area narcotics squad, said he had no knowledge of her being an informant. Detectives Clarence Jobe and Charles Swartfager, who were also assigned to the case, also denied it.

Around the time of Diane's murder, several people connected to the Den Massage Parlor were arrested in what was called one of the biggest cocaine busts in Iowa. At least one of the defendants retained the same attorney Diane had used. I have always wondered, was that simply a coincidence? Or was there anger over Diane taking choice clients away and keeping records? Maybe they weren't convinced the attorney had talked her out of becoming an informant, and blamed her for their arrests.

Diane was only twenty-one at the time, and really had no one she could look to for guidance. She was likely very naïve when it came to the realities of the lifestyle she was living.

While this was going on in Diane's life, I was eighteen years old and had a one-year-old child of my own. Not being old enough to get into bars and being responsible for my own child, our lives were quite different. Diane never told me anything about the massage business or being approached to be an informant. I was pretty much oblivious as to what was happening with her. To my mind, we were both having the time of our lives. We were young, and other than both having young children, I thought we were carefree. Diane moved into a new apartment and had several roommates, both male and female. She seemed to be enjoying her life.

One of the things we loved doing together was to go swimming at our favorite lake, Clear Water Beach. On July 4, 1975, Diane was scheduled to go to work at Dave Salem's bar in the evening, so we went to the lake in the afternoon for some sun and fun. In the water we floated on rubber rafts Diane brought in the trunk of her car, a tan 1966 Rambler. As we floated, we talked and held hands to keep from drifting apart. Some of her friends were there, too, including William Smith and his nephew Dan Casin. Diane was going to give them a ride home. As we said our goodbyes, I told Diane how much fun I'd had, and we promised to get together again soon.

I did not see or hear from Diane for a few days but didn't think much about it. I figured she was doing her own thing and had no reason to be concerned.

On Thursday, July 10, I went to my older brother Kenny's house, and he had not heard from Diane either. Still, I wasn't worried. I went back home and while watching TV, a breaking news story came on that the body of a Des Moines woman had been found in the trunk of a car parked at Warrens Steak House, near the Des Moines airport. A picture flashed of a flatbed truck hauling away Diane's tan Rambler. I was stunned. The dead person couldn't be Diane. That wasn't possible. For a moment I honestly thought maybe Diane had killed somebody, and that was whose body had been found. I thought that no matter what she had done, we would get through it together. And then my brother called and reality set in.

A police officer had knocked on his door, gave him a business card and told him to call the number on it. It was a local funeral home. They had Diane's body and her car. Our sister was dead.

When my brother and I got to the funeral home, neither of our parents were there. Diane's car was in the basement and her body was lying on the floor beside it. At first, we weren't allowed to see her, but a staff member assured us the body they had was Diane's. He left only to return with a different story. Perhaps she had loaned her car and insurance card to a friend to go to a dentist appointment. Maybe it wasn't Diane, after all. He went away again returned saying the dead person was Diane, and this time there was no doubt. Remember, this conflicting information was all from funeral home personnel. Police detectives had not yet spoken with us.

Everyone was telling me that I didn't want to see her, but I did want to. Had I been more mature, I would have simply walked around the car to look at her body. I was intimidated, though, and stayed put.

The funeral director then came out with a Styrofoam cup and emptied its contents on the table. Diane's new watch and several of her rings were there, indicating robbery was not the motive for the murder. That, and a statement from her dentist, was how Diane's body was initially identified.

My brother and I were never allowed to see the body. In fact, no one in my family saw her. Over the years, I've tried to imagine what she looked like and sought to see the police photos of her body. It took forty-two years of begging before police showed me the pictures.

I was interviewed by police the night Diane's body was found. Other than that, the only contacts I've had with the police have been initiated by me. Her case remains an unsolved homicide.

When Diane was murdered, it all seemed so surreal at first. Why would anyone kill my sweet, fun-loving sister? At the time, police said she had been strangled with a towel, which seemed so odd to me. But after obtaining her autopsy report, I came to understand that it was a towel which had been torn into strips and triple knotted. After tying her up with it, her assailant strangled Diane and put her in the trunk of her own car. When she was finally discovered, she was so badly decomposed, her family could never see her again, not even to say goodbye.

I waited for an arrest to be made. Days turned into weeks, then months, and then years. It has now been over four decades, and no one has been charged.

In the beginning, everything I learned about Diane's death and the investigation came from newspaper accounts and talking to people on the streets. Later, I started calling the detective assigned to her case, and all the others who followed him. I have talked to police chiefs, spokespersons, secretaries, and everyone in between. I've been treated mostly in a condescending manner, sometimes worse—belligerent and rude. Some inferred that when a person lived the lifestyle Diane did, that is what happens to them. Her murder was her own fault.

In addition to dealing with the police, I have initiated newspaper and TV interviews, held vigils, marched at the courthouse, launched a letter-writing campaign to the district attorney. He responded to all the letters from Iowans that he had never heard of the case. Letters from out of state were not acknowledged at all.

In my yard is a four-foot by four-foot sign with Diane's picture, date of death, and the fact that the case remains unsolved. I live on a very busy four-lane street, so the sign gets a lot of attention. I also have a Facebook group for her with over 1,200 members.

Because Diane was found in the trunk of her own car, I assume someone drove her car to the dumping spot, and someone had to give them a ride from there. Someone must have seen something, yet no one has come forward with information. Des Moines is not a large town. Who are these people who have gained the silence of an entire town for forty-three years?

I have come to doubt that there is such a thing as justice, and believe closure is nothing but a myth—it does not exist. I do believe in accountability, though, and that her killer has to be identified, even if he is now dead himself. I've repeatedly told police that if there is a valid reason someone can't be named due to a lack of evidence, tell me and I will let it go. But they insist it is an open case and still being worked.

Every lead I have ever gotten—and there are many—I've given to the police. I have given them names of people who say they know who killed Diane. Two sisters came to me and stated they were so sure their father was responsible that they would submit DNA tests and help raise money to pay for the tests. They called the police themselves to talk about it and left a message. They were never called back.

A woman called and told me she had been staying at Diane's apartment for a few days, and was with her the night of July 4. She said she saw Diane leave the bar with a man, and described both the guy and what Diane was wearing that night. I told the police and gave them the woman's contact information. They never contacted her.

I've given the police many leads, but as far as I know they haven't followed through on any. They have told me virtually nothing. No regular or even periodic updates. They have never called me or my family. It has always been us reaching out to them. Both my parents have died, never knowing who killed their daughter.

Over the years a couple detectives said a man named Raul Ancer, now deceased, was hired to kill Diane. He was also a suspect in another murder-for-hire. That victim, Lillian Randolph, was also found fully clothed in the trunk of her car at the Des Moines airport, across the street from where Diane was found. Her purse was on the front seat, so robbery was not suspected. In spite of the similarities, Ancer was not named as Diane's killer.

In 2015, I began speaking with Detective Matt Towers about Diane's case. He assured me it was open and active. The only new information he has given me is that early on, one person was given a lie detector test and that there was DNA from the strips of towel that had been tested in 2010. Nothing further.

When the two sisters offered to have their DNA tested and I wanted Parabon Lab to do the testing, Towers said there was only enough left of the sample to do one more test. I thought when you ran DNA you got a profile, which could be tested again and again, but maybe I'm wrong on that.

In 2015, I contacted retired detective Clarence Jobe and asked if there was anything he could tell me. To my surprise, he said, "Yes, I will tell you who killed your sister."

Jobe gave me a name and told me where the man had worked—at the very hotel the towels used to bind Diane were traced to. He said he was so sure this man was the murderer that he had submitted his name to the district attorney, twice. Both times the DA declined to act, citing lack of evidence. This was the same DA who later claimed he had never heard of Diane's case.

I called Towers the next day and told him what I had learned from Jobe. Towers said he would look into it. A few days later I called Jobe to ask a question, and he politely said he didn't have any more answers and not to call again. Two weeks later, he did admit to Lee Root, a reporter with the Des Moines Register, that he had given me that information because he felt sorry for me. That is the closest I have ever come to having an honest conversation with Des Moines police.

There are many more things I could say about the investigation into Diane's death. However, I don't want to divulge anything that could compromise the supposedly ongoing police investigation. I understand there may be some things the police can't share, but any information from them would be welcomed. Please, talk to me. Be honest, that's all I ask.

When my sister was murdered, I was sentenced to a life of grief. I will get no days off for good behavior—there will be no early release. I will serve every day of my sentence. Not a day goes by that I don't think about her and wonder who killed her.

TWYLA DALTON JOHNSON, Diane's sister

None of the main issues which humanity is facing
will be resolved without access to information.

—CHRISTOPHE DELOIRE
Reporters Without Borders

CHAPTER SEVENTEEN

Mariah Wine & Hank Few

BY DONNA FEW
Mariah and Hank's mom

On Thursday, June 14, 2012, at around 10:30, Teddy, my daughter's partner and the father of her three children, called and said that Mariah was lying on the floor, dead. I need to point out that Teddy had been arrested four times over the years for assaulting Mariah. On one of those  arrests, Teddy held a gun to her head prior to her giving birth to their second child. He also burned down the house accidentally while she and the children were asleep. The baby woke them up and they managed to get out just before the house exploded.

I had spoken with Mariah the day before she died. She told me she was sick and didn't know what was wrong. I asked her to call an ambulance and go to a hospital. She replied that Teddy said they couldn't afford the medical expenses, so she wasn't going to seek treatment. Eventually, Mariah and I worked out a plan where I would come get her on Thursday after I was finished for the day on my farm, and take her to the hospital.

On Tuesday, two days before, I saw her at a meeting in Brevard, North Carolina. She was so out of it, she could barely walk. I told her brother Hank to take her home. Later, he told me that when he went to pick up Mariah for the meeting that morning, he couldn't wake her. He said her lips were blue, and so were her feet. He said he went into the kitchen and when he came back, Teddy was by her bed giving her one of his prescription pills. Teddy is a paraplegic and has strong medications for pain, including methadone and Xanax.

After Hank took her home from the meeting, I tried calling her the rest of the day, but she would not answer the phone. I called the Transylvania County Sheriff's Office (TCSO) and asked them to do a wellness check on her. When they called me back, they said all the lights were on and both Mariah and Teddy were asleep, but they were able to wake them, and everything was apparently okay.

On Wednesday, I wasn't able to get an answer to my calls until around 2:30 p.m. That was when we had the conversation about calling an ambulance. Late that evening I spoke with Mariah again, and confirmed I would pick her up and take her to the hospital. Before that could happen, I received the call from Teddy saying she was dead.

Here is the timeline starting from when I received Teddy's call.

10:30 — Call from Teddy.

11:30 — Teddy called a neighbor to come to his house. The neighbor stated Mariah was cold and dead.

11:54 — Teddy called EMS. Mariah was pronounced dead and her body removed for autopsy.

According to the autopsy report, Teddy told TCSO that Mariah had argued with me the previous night, and said she would kill herself. What I found even more shocking is that Teddy also claimed Mariah had been sick and her lips were blue while she was sleeping, but she refused medical care because of costs and lack of insurance. He further stated that he checked her pulse at 8 a.m. and a pulse was present. He checked again at 11 a.m. and found no pulse. He attempted CPR and then called emergency services.

The EMS report states that a medic noticed possible bruising of the neck when starting evaluation. Teddy stated there were no drugs in the house other than Cymbalta.

The autopsy's major findings were, "acute hypoxic ischemic brain injury, early aspiration pneumonia and urinary retention, which can be seen with acute or sprite and benzo intoxication."

Following Mariah's death, my sons Hank and Dodgen moved into Teddy's house to help with the children and do errands for him. Little did I know that Hank suspected Teddy had murdered his sister, and that was the real reason he was there. I know now that Hank informed Teddy, "If the toxicology reports come back with your medications in my sister's blood, you and I are on."

On August 28, we got Mariah's toxicology report. It stated that the cause of death was mixed drug (methadone, alprazolam) toxicity. I found the following text messages on Mariah's phone from the day before she died:

> 12:37 — I love you too keep your head up there is every reason in the world to get it together
>
> 2:17 — Just woke up Mom is going to come tomorrow and take me to the hospital
>
> 2:27 — I've got a virus, or something feel like I am dying retain fluid and shit
>
> 2:29 — I'm swollen
>
> 2:33 — Mom wants to take me up to the mountain (hospital) but would rather go to town IDK don't feel like moving at all
>
> 2:53 — I am trying not to go (emergency room) I just want everyone to leave me alone and let me get over it
>
> 3:30 — IDK I blew Mom off I feel better, but I still can't eat
>
> 3:38 — If you saw me you'd swear someone blacked my eyes I look and feel like shit

TCSO had Mariah's phone for over eight months, and refused my request to have it returned until I called the supervisor.

I am sure now that Mariah did not commit suicide. I regret that I was not able to handle the truth when Hank called and told me, "Teddy just admitted to killing Mariah." After that admission, Teddy kicked Hank out of the house. If I had been in better shape mentally at that time, maybe Hank would still be alive.

TCSO did not do an investigation of Mariah's death. They never called or questioned me, not even to ask if Mariah had threatened to kill herself. If they had, I would have answered, "Absolutely not." The drugs she overdosed on were Teddy's, and he was seen giving her pills two days before she died, yet they took his word for everything and didn't look any further. To claim her death was investigated is a joke.

On October 11, just after 3 p.m., I got a phone call from one of Hank's friends. "Donna, Hank is missing. He's been gone for two days."

I immediately left work and started driving to where Hank was last seen. It was a friend's house he moved into after Teddy evicted him from his house. On my way I called the sheriff's office and made a missing person report. Deputies arrived shortly thereafter.

There were eight people there when I arrived. According to the deputies, the story they were told by the witnesses was that Hank was upset because it was the eve of his sister's thirtieth birthday, and he wandered off into the woods. I immediately noticed that Hank's dog was there and knew the dog would have gone with Hank if he had actually walked off into the woods. Also, he supposedly left behind his brand-new cell phone, cigarettes, lighter and pocket knife. No way. The two deputies were suspicious, too.

There were four fire trucks there, two rescue squad vehicles and Gorges State Park (GSP) Search Rescue, gathered in preparation for a search, and around thirty people waiting for orders to get started.

Deputy Seth Queen was in charge at the scene (he would later be named in my wrongful death suit). When his first cousin, Detective Jeremy Queen, arrived, Seth took one of the female witnesses I'll call

KK, to his car, where they spoke in private. He then got out of his car and announced the search had been called off. When I questioned him about why he canceled the search, he answered, "That's like searching for a needle in a haystack."

Seth stood in front of the house until after dark. Not once did he walk around or even look around, he just stood there watching me. He told me before he left that they would be back in the morning and begin searching then. I stayed until around 2 a.m. and returned at daylight, but nobody showed up to search.

I went to GSP State Park and spoke with the man who had been in charge of the rescue team the night before. He told me he was waiting to hear from the sheriff's office, and had expected them to call way before then. They finally called and did fly a helicopter over at around 3 p.m. But when they spotted a marijuana patch, they got distracted and lost interest in finding Hank.

I spent that whole day asking questions and looking around the property until way past dark. Around 6 p.m. I went into the house to retrieve Hank's clothes. Inside I met a guy named Jim, whom I had never met before. He asked what I knew about Hank's relationship with KK. I told him I knew Hank had been dating her for a few weeks, but I had not met her. Jim told me a guy I'll call Marty had been having an affair with KK behind Hank's back, and Marty had murdered Hank by injecting him with bad dope.

Later that evening, I called Jeremy Queen and told him I was sure Hank was dead. I begged him to get cadaver dogs and conduct a search.

He replied that he was sorry but since it was the weekend, he couldn't do that.

The next day, October 13, I arrived by myself to search for Hank. Around 3 p.m. I saw a pair of silk boxer shorts by the creek, beside them were fresh footprints that weren't there the day before, leading into the laurel thicket. I followed the footprints for about fifty yards and found Hank in a mudpuddle of stagnant water, but he was not submerged. He was dead. His arm was folded up behind his back and he was covered in mud. How did he get all the mud on him? Why, when the coroner got him, did his clothes have to be cut off because he had inches of mud on his back? Why was there mud in his trachea? In his ears? Why was his mouth full of mud? All that mud, yet he was not underwater.

I called the sheriff's office to report what I'd found. When the first deputy arrived on scene, he walked on nearly every footprint near Hank's body. I said, "You're walking on all those footprints."

"Oh, it doesn't matter. They know what our boot prints look like," he replied.

After walking over the footprints, the deputy told me I was going to have to leave Hank's body. I had been sitting there just looking at him for the thirty or so minutes it took the sheriff's deputy to arrive. He then threatened to arrest me if I didn't leave.

Jeremy Queen and several others then showed up. By then, crime scene tape had been put up and I'd been told to stay where I was and not move. I told Jeremy not to touch Hank's body until the State Bureau of Investigation (SBI) arrived. He argued that I wasn't allowed to call the SBI. That's when a deputy pulled me aside and said, "Donna, you're allowed to request SBI and if I were you, I would insist." Which is what I did.

It was hours before SBI arrived. In the meantime, deputies were stationed around the property, standing guard. Before SBI arrived, Hank's head mysteriously moved from sideways to face down. I know that, because I've seen the photos SBI took.

In spite of all the unexplained questions, the investigation failed to result in Hank's death being ruled a homicide. Someone was getting away with murder.

In the days after I found Hank's body, I began to hear many stories about what really happened to Hank. I called the sheriff's office many times to ask questions, but they wouldn't return my phone calls. That's when I started emailing.

My uncle, a retired judge, a family friend, and I met with one of the detectives on October 24. He promised to let us see the SBI photos and return Hank's personal effects. He never did.

Knowing there was little chance of getting justice through the police, I filed a civil wrongful death suit against ten people I believed were involved in Hank's death. As part of that suit, in January 2016, I was able to obtain copies of the sheriff's office and State Bureau of Investigation files. Hank's body was not where I found it when I searched that area the two days prior. In the sheriff's file there was a statement from a next-door neighbor saying that the night before I found Hank, he saw a truck pull up to the spot where I found him. It stayed fifteen to twenty minutes, and then left. Another neighbor's statement in the file states he and his dogs were in that very area the previous night, and Hank wasn't there.

The State Bureau of Investigation file shows a more thorough investigation than the sheriff's office. Documents in their file indicate they felt Hank's death was, in fact, a homicide. It wasn't until almost four years later that Hank's clothes and wallet were returned to us as part of the wrongful death suit.

Shockingly, in the sheriff's office file was an audio recording of a detective speaking with a former Polk County deputy. The recording was received only five days after I found Hank's body. The deputy told the detective that his daughter had knowledge of Hank's murder. He said, "She said she witnessed it."

In response to this admission the detective said, "Well, even if she witnessed it, it's called accessory after the fact or accessory during the fact or whatever and still whoever gets—you know, wants to come forth first."

This statement can be interpreted as an attempt on the part of the detective to cover up and suppress this evidence, particularly in light of the fact that the detective and his partner squirreled the recording of this conversation away in such a manner that it was only discovered in the discovery process of the lawsuit.

This conclusion is bolstered by the fact that in February 2013, one of those detectives was asked by SBI agent Tom Ammons if he had any more evidence regarding Hank's death. He answered, "No."

My fight for justice goes on and I will not rest until I get it.

DONNA FEW, Mariah and Hank's mom

CHAPTER EIGHTEEN

Samantha Carolyn Sutton

BY DELL SUTTON
Sam's mom

On March 25, 2011, my twenty-two-year-old daughter Samantha was transported by Carroll County, Georgia Sheriff's officers to Cobb County, where she was court-ordered into the Cobb-Douglas CSB, Dual Diagnosis Program by the Carroll County Drug Court.

Sam was to complete six months as a drug court participant. Upon completion, all charges against her would be dropped.

Sam was arrested at age eighteen while in the company of a man named Benjamin Derrick Richardson, who was in his mid-twenties. This individual's name appears in the records of the National Center for Missing & Exploited Children (NCMEC) as a perpetrator with family members in law enforcement. Sam was charged with four felony drug offenses. Richardson suffered no consequences for his actions, though. He was allowed to become a cooperating witness for state prosecutors, and received a pass for his activities with Sam.

Upon her arrest, the authorities confiscated what was left of the money Sam received as settlement from a car accident when she was riding with a man named Brad Denmond.

Denmond had been arrested in Haralson County, Georgia, a year earlier while with Sam who, at the time, was listed as a missing and exploited child. However, authorities took no further action against Denmond, and in my opinion, this was just another example of the authorities throwing Sam under the bus. When dealing with her, it seemed as though law enforcement didn't think she was of much value and not worth expending a lot of energy on.

I have mountains of documentation to support those beliefs and other conclusions I have reached while trying to get to the bottom of the circumstances surrounding Sam's death. They include court records, medical records, Sam's handwritten notes, police records and reports and witness statements.

When Samantha arrived at the drug treatment facility, I was allowed to bring her some clothes and other items she would need for the living quarters she would be sharing with two other participants. I got to see her room and help decorate it. We walked around the complex, saw the pool, and did a lot of girl talk. She seemed so happy and at ease. I was optimistic that she would finally be able to put her horrid past behind her.

Things went very well for a few weeks. Sam was working the program, adjusting well, and making new friends. She seemed happier than I had seen her in a very long time.

Her dad, sister and I planned to visit her on April 17. I was about to walk out the door to go to the facility when I received a call from Sam saying I didn't need to come, there was a change of plans. Kevin Griffin, her former boyfriend, was coming instead. She asked me not to tell her dad or brother about Kevin, and said I could bring more of her personal stuff to her the next day. With that call, my optimism was dashed. The old dread and fear returned, and my worst nightmare began to unfold.

Kevin should not have been allowed to visit Sam. According to records and witness statements I subsequently obtained, he brought drugs and alcohol to her and even talked her into leaving the facility to spend the night with him. When Sam returned the next morning, she was confronted by Dewanna Belton, coordinator of the rehab program. A drug test was ordered, and Sam failed it. The police and Carroll County drug court coordinator were notified. At that point, Samantha panicked and ran. I wasn't informed about all this until the following morning. Instead of delivering more stuff to her, I was told to come and remove her property.

I contacted Sam's lawyer, Bob Cullen. He was already aware of everything that had happened and was working on making sure Sam was safe and getting her back into the program. None of that happened.

On April 30, at approximately 11:37 a.m., my phone rang. It was an officer with the Carroll County Sheriff's Office (CCSO). There had been an accident, he said. Sam had overdosed at Kevin's apartment. She was being transported by ambulance to the Tanner Medical Center (TMC) in Carrollton. I questioned the officer further about Sam's condition. He finally said, "Your daughter is dead."

I called Sam's dad, who lived close to the hospital, her sister in Memphis, and my mom. I then called the hospital. They told me it was okay to come, that I would be able to see Sam. I was about an hour and a half away.

When I arrived, her dad was already there. He said that when he got there, he was immediately escorted to the morgue by two hospital guards. He identified Sam's body, held her, and prayed for her. He described her as being warm to the touch, she had color, and looked as if she was asleep. He thought she would wake up any minute. He then went to the lobby to wait for me.

It was a different story for me, however. I was told I couldn't see Sam. She had been tagged and bagged, and was being turned over to the Georgia Bureau of Investigation. I was shocked! I pleaded with everyone in authority, but to no avail. I was not allowed to see her.

Sam's funeral was horrific. Many of the drug dealers who were arrested with her—and in my opinion, were supplying her—showed up and interrupted the service. Her father and I had alerted law enforcement of that possibility and requested security. As usual, they were of no help. I couldn't even bury my daughter in peace!

On April 30, I spoke with Sammy Eady, an investigator with the sheriff's office. He assured me they were investigating Sam's death and would get to the bottom of what happened. In my opinion, his promise turned out to be a joke.

Over the next few days, I spoke with Eady. He told me he had not gone to the scene (Kevin's apartment) or interviewed Kevin. He added that it was his understanding that Kevin had been on the phone with the sheriff's office for thirty minutes prior to placing a 9-1-1 call for assistance, and that GBI would handle the investigation. I called the GBI and was given a case number.

I again contacted Eady and asked him to get the reports from the sheriff's office, Fair Field Fire Department, West Georgia Ambulance Service, and Tanner Medical Center, which I'd already obtained. In the records, I found a DOA Initial Assessment dated April 30, entered by an R.N. that read, "Time: 12:50. Body brought in by coroner, not viewed by hospital staff."

However, Eady's report says he wasn't notified of Sam's death until 1:08 p.m., eighteen minutes after he supposedly delivered her body to the hospital. Unfortunately, this was the beginning of a disturbing pattern of contradictory statements and reports that cause me to doubt the reliability of any of the accounts and the credibility of the individuals or agencies who prepared them.

My journey to find the truth has been long and arduous. Contacting people who may have information, making open record requests, and doing other research has taxed me to the limit. In spite of that, I have made some progress and reached a conclusion. I do not believe my daughter was dead on April 30, 2011. I'll explain my reasons below. But first I need to tell you the tools I used to get there.

First and foremost, I learned to keep detailed notes of who I've spoken with and what was said. They have been a godsend as I move forward, and I refer to them continuously. I also obtained a Georgia Law Enforcement Handbook, which has been invaluable. My sister helped me by downloading and printing the entire Georgia Open Records file and other documents, as well as helping me organize my files and preserving them on flash drives. In addition, I have a brother-in-law with law enforcement experience who helped open my eyes. His reaction after reviewing the relevant materials was, "What kind of an investigation is this?"

Now, here are specific reasons why I am skeptical of the accounts of Sam's death as given by the authorities. The second time I called the GBI, they didn't have a record of Samantha Carolyn Sutton. Thank God I had her case number. Through the open records act, I found they had listed her name as Samantha Caroline Dutton.

After her death, I contacted Poison Control of Georgia and asked them to take a look at Sam's toxicology report and render an opinion. They told me, "None of the drugs present, individually or together, caused Samantha's death."

In fact, the CD I obtained from GBI contained a statement by their chief medical examiner, Dr. Sperry, made to me during a phone conversation: "[Sam] ...would have died within three to four minutes of receiving the shot." This made me realize that Sam could not have been dead on April 29, at 10:30 p.m.

I began to review the Quantitation Report:

- Mepivacaine 1.00 mcg/L (an anesthetic that can numb an area of the body to relieve pain during surgery or a medical procedure).

- Nalorphine 1.00 mcg/L (a mixed opioid agonist-antagonist with opioid antagonist and analgesic properties).

- Cocaine 50.14 mcg/L (shown in the toxicology report as).

- Codeine 48.11 mcg/L (a controlled substance/narcotic that can cause respiratory distress and death when taken in high doses or combined with other substances).

- Morphine 249.07 mcg/L (narcotic/controlled substance that can cause respiratory distress and death when taken in high doses).

Nalorphine is a narcotic that produces a spectrum of unpleasant effects when given alone, and is considered to be clinically obsolete. How did it get into her system on May 2, if she was decomposing in the morgue on April 30? The toxicology report was requested by the sheriff's office. The blood specimen used for the test was drawn by Dr. Eason on May 2, for testing on May 3. Dr. Eason's report dated July 7, noted the following:

Submission 002B

1. positive, citalopram, 0.35 mg/L
2. positive, alprazolam
3. positive, cocaine, 50 ..../L
4. positive, benzoylecgonine, 0.89 mg/L
5. positive, morphine, 0.24 mg/L

Only those items discussed in the results above were analyzed for this report. The above represents the interpretations of the undersigned analyst. Evidence analyzed in this report will be returned to the submitting agency. .... Technical notes and data supporting the conclusions and findings in this report are maintained within the laboratory case records.

At some point, Eady brought Sam's body (or person) into the hospital in Villa Rica. We know it could not have been on April 30, because she was in the morgue at the hospital in Carrollton, at that time being held by her father. He took photos. Someone drew blood on May 3, but there is no chain of custody for it. When the GBI took photos of Sam's body on May 2, she had color, a flat stomach, moist lips, moist mucus membranes, her breast were full Ds, not flat as they were in Eady's photos. Why the multicolor bruises she had were not photographed remains a mystery.

It's clear that not all this information can be accurate. Records show that Samantha did not leave the hospital until 1800 on April 30, when she was transported to the GBI. How many places could she have been at the same time? The inconsistencies are too numerous to be attributed to simple typos.

There are additional questions, as well. Sammy Eady's report says Sam was found deceased at the Villas on South Lakeview Drive in Villa Rica. If true, why do records show that all emergency response units were dispatched to 322 Berry Court? And why were the lines for FINDER'S NAME, ADDRESS, PHONE, DATE and TIME, LAST KNOWN ALIVE and WITNESS'S NAME, ADDRESS, PHONE all left blank, even though the form requires they be completed if the decedent is found dead?

Reports show that the coroner was not on the scene, although he was mandated by law to respond. Why wasn't he there? The law says, "No person shall move or authorize the removal of any body from the place where the same is found until the investigation is completed, and such removal is authorized by the coroner or medical examiner is present at such investigation."

The EMTs violated that law by removing Sam's body prior to an investigation. Why?

When a person is found deceased and the death was unattended or under suspicious or unusual circumstances, the law requires an investigation by the coroner or medical examiner. There was no coroner's investigation, inquiry, or inquest in Sam's case. Why?

Kevin Griffin called 9-1-1 to report he thought his girlfriend was dead at 11:05 on April 30. The call lasted a little over six minutes. However, it turned out there was another call. I found that out when I listened to the in-car video I received through open records, and heard Kevin say he had dropped his phone and had called back. That means he had two conversations with the authorities, and the other call was initially undisclosed. Why? Was it intentional?

When I was finally able to hear it, Kevin was heard saying that Sam was breathing. The call was dispatched that way. He also admitted to taking her to buy drugs, and admitted to cleaning up the scene. He failed to get her immediate medical attention, tampered with evidence, and violated the Georgia Drug Dealer's Liability Act. If Sam was in fact dead at the scene, Kevin should have been arrested and charged with homicide. He wasn't even charged with a probation violation and walked away unscathed. How could that be?

There are two different versions of Sam's death certificate. One states she died in the emergency room at Tanner Medical Center as an outpatient. The other said she died as an inpatient. Neither of them agrees with the coroner's report that Sam was found dead at the Villas. Why?

I believe these and other questions fully justify my skepticism. I am confident that the hundreds of pages of documents, photos, and other records I've collected will prove me right.

So, I will continue to seek justice for my daughter, regardless of the myriad roadblocks I continue to encounter. I won't stop or give up until all my questions are answered.

DELL SUTTON, Sam's mom

CHAPTER NINETEEN

Kathy Lynn Gloddy

BY KAREN BEAUDIN
Kathy's sister

Writing about Kathy's murder is hard. November 21, 2018, marked forty-seven years that her case has gone unsolved—forty-seven years of missing her.

Kathy Lynn Gloddy
13 Years Old
Murdered November 21, 1971

My sister Kathy was thirteen when she was murdered in the small town of Franklin, New Hampshire. Kathy was beaten, raped (possibly multiple times), strangled, and left naked in the woods approximately three miles from our home. Her body was run over several times, the killer wanted to make sure she was dead. Her murder is still unsolved.

The case was reactivated in 1983, and again in 2004. In 2006, Kathy's remains were exhumed for DNA but because her grave had been compromised, DNA was unobtainable. The initial cover was broken into pieces, and debris covered her inside the vault. She had been exposed to the elements, her casket disintegrated. Someone had installed a new vault cover which led detectives to believe everything was intact and in good condition to obtain DNA. It was yet another disappointment, one of many we've experienced over the years.

The day after Kathy went missing, I went to look for her on the railroad tracks by our home. I had hoped to find a clue. It was a short-cut we often took to the convenience store where she was seen the night before. She would never stay out all night without telling someone where she was. When I returned home, my mother sat in a chair crying, and a doctor stood over her with a syringe.

My sister Janet sat on the arm of the chair next to her. My father stood to the right of Janet, and he too was crying. There were police officers in the room. My grandmother stood next to my mom and looked confused. I asked, "Why is everyone crying?" That's when Janet told me Kathy had been found. She was dead, murdered.

I couldn't believe it. "No, it's not true," I said over and over again. I went into the kitchen, put my face into a corner and sobbed. My grandmother came in and pointed her finger at me. "Stop that crying; you're going to upset your mother," she said. From that day on, I cried mostly alone.

The initial shock was excruciating. Life was empty. The grief was truly indescribable. I walked among the living but felt dead. The following days were about motion. When I was told to move, I did; when I was told to speak, I did. I couldn't grasp that Kathy wasn't coming home, never mind that she had been murdered. My mind was full of questions. What happened? How could this be? They must be wrong! Please let them be wrong!

Kathy's funeral was a traditional one that included three days of viewing and then a mass. My siblings and I made the funeral decisions. My parents couldn't function. My sisters Ann and Janet bought a dress for Kathy, a tomboy who was in the early stages of becoming a young woman. The dress had daisies on it, Kathy's favorite flower. But the funeral director called and said he couldn't use it; the dress had to have long sleeves and a very high neckline to hide her injuries.

On the first day of the viewing, we were ready to go to the funeral home when the funeral director called again. He said law enforcement had taken Kathy's body back for some tests. We canceled the first day of the viewing. Decades later, we found out that new bruising appeared on Kathy's body and photos needed to be taken.

The following day, the funeral director told us we could still have a closed casket. He said he had done the best he could but some of the bruises were still visible. My mother was adamant about having an open casket. When I saw Kathy, I was traumatized. It didn't look like her. The heavy makeup and the way her hair was placed looked unnatural. It's an image I'll never forget. I understand my mother's request for an open casket, but I wish I hadn't seen Kathy that way.

Hundreds of people came to the Catholic Mass. School buses transported adults and children to attend. The church was full. It was heartwarming to know so many were there for Kathy. After the mass, they came to the cemetery. It was cold and windy.

Originally, the caretaker of the cemetery told us Kathy would need to be buried in the spring. My mother was distraught. The thought of another service in the spring was devastating. To save my family from the anguish of a spring memorial, the caretaker agreed to bury Kathy in November.

Every day was hard after Kathy was found murdered. Every minute was grim. Getting up in the morning was just as difficult as going to bed at night. I thought this kind of grief would never end. It was unfathomable to think I'd ever be happy again. If I slept, it was intermittent. With morning came the reality that Kathy had been murdered, I wished I could erase it all. As time went on, bedtime was the most excruciating. I shared a room with Kathy, and not having her in the same space was a constant reminder that she was never coming home. Her absence ached like nothing I'd ever felt before.

The effects from a cold case linger for life. Fear of the unknown forces the mind to travel down the road of imagination, tormenting the already tormented mind. As a child, I was afraid of being alone. I wouldn't take a shower unless someone was home. I didn't close my eyes, even when I rinsed shampoo out of my hair. Making sure the doors were bolted and windows latched became a nightly ritual. Darkness elevated my imagination and anxiety. I was afraid to walk alone, something I did all the time before Kathy was murdered.

The first day I returned to school was dreadful. I felt like an outsider. Many firsts were just as painful. The first Thanksgiving, Christmas, and Kathy's birthday were but a few. The seconds and thirds were painful, too. I wondered if it would always be that way. As years passed, grief hit in waves. I came to the realization that I would always grieve her. Not in the way it was early on, which was constant with no relief, but in moments of time. I would be sad and cry, but it was okay. Releasing that sorrow was much better than keeping it all inside. My tears were a sign of love, not weakness. I will always miss Kathy. To me, moving on was learning to live without her and with the knowledge that she was murdered.

When leads have been exhausted, an investigation is considered a cold case. When a case is considered cold, families stop receiving information. This lack of information adds to their grief.

As a survivor I want people to know there is hope. Kathy was only thirteen when she was murdered, and I was barely fifteen. During that time, I needed someone to tell me there was hope. I needed to know that the torment I felt would not always be this agonizing.

It took decades before I could tell Kathy's story, reach out to others and use my years of experience to encourage law enforcement to never give up on unsolved cases. I began to heal in a different way. It was my way to honor her.

At age fifteen, the media was evil to me. They were intrusive and didn't seem to care about the pain my family was in. In one instance, a reporter came to our home and asked me to sit on the front steps with Kathy's dog, Tasha. Tasha was with Kathy the night she disappeared. I thought, I hate you. I was tormented by Kathy's murder, and all they wanted was a story. I'll never forget it.

I later learned to appreciate the media and how they can bring a cold case back into the public's eye. The media can be a thorn in one's side, but they can also be a lifeline in keeping a case active. Over the years I've learned to work with them, and encourage others seeking justice to use the media to help bring attention to their own case.

Every journey is different. I speak to criminal justice students at universities and to law enforcement officers about the long-term effects of cold cases. Murder follows a family for the rest of their lives. I found a way to take the tragic circumstance and do something positive to help others. This helps in the healing process. I believe I'll always be in the process of healing.

My faith has directed my path, though it wasn't always that way. I searched for a purpose in life, and for the longest time I couldn't find it. It's terrible to wander and feel like you don't belong anywhere. I was able to see ways in which I could honor Kathy with love and in the work I do. I opened my heart to change, and to make a difference in Kathy's name.

What happened to Kathy has reached across the United States, Canada, the United Kingdom, and even Japan. When I hear from others about how Kathy's story has influenced them, it's encouraging.

Forgiveness is personal. It allows me to be constructive in the way I honor Kathy. Early on, I made the decision not to hate every law enforcement officer because of one who was corrupt. I strive not to be suspicious of all because of one who murdered. I won't be defeated because of one who seeks to defeat me. And I choose not to let a murderer take all my happiness. If I do, he's won twofold: He murdered my sister and has also taken my life. I may have physical life, but I won't truly be alive. So in effect, he has destroyed both of us.

Forgiveness does not mean the murderer should go free; I still believe he should pay for what he did to Kathy. He committed a crime. Forgiveness has nothing to do with that.

Hope comes in many forms, seen and unseen. I've seen it in a daisy, Kathy's favorite flower. I've watched it in a butterfly that has appeared in the most unusual place or time. Hope is in the sparrow that followed me home during a time I thought I'd never find my wings again. I believe God sent these reminders to show me He cares, and to remind me to keep my eyes open for future promises. Hope comes in the form of baby steps or giant leaps.

I have honored Kathy in simple ways, too. I've sent a message tied to a balloon. I've given someone a daisy, helped a person in need, and given a hardworking waitress a larger tip. I've made donations to organizations Kathy would have supported.

I miss Kathy. There will always be times when a place, picture, person, or even a smell triggers a memory of her. I may cry, and that's okay. I no longer let anyone make me feel guilty when I need to grieve her loss. There's not a right or wrong way to fight through the grieving process. And fight we must, it is a battle. Never give up.

KAREN BEAUDIN, Kathy's sister

Integrity, transparency and the fight against corruption have to be part of the culture. They have to be taught as fundamental values.

ANGEL GURRIA
OECD Secretary General

CHAPTER TWENTY

Heidi M. Allen

BY LISA M. BUSKE
Heidi's sister

Thank you for taking time to read about my sister, Heidi M. Allen, and her case. I want to start by letting you know that when I hear "cold case," I shudder because I never want my sister's kidnapping case to be cold.

Heidi was kidnapped, on April 3, 1994, Easter Sunday, from New Haven, New York. This is a small town in Oswego County, bordering Lake Ontario. Heidi went to work on Easter Sunday so a colleague could stay home to see her children find their Easter baskets. Heidi rang her last transaction at 7:42 a.m. and remains missing at the time of this book's publication.

I understand the meaning of cold case and how my sister's case is cold because she remains missing after twenty-five years. But when I think of the dedication of the Oswego County Sheriff's Department and the Oswego District Attorney's office, Heidi's case is only cold by a societal norm that when someone has been missing for a decade or more, the case is cold. A case is cold because the next generation of officers has forgotten about the case and moved it to the back of a filing cabinet. A case is cold when no leads or follow-up are made to law enforcement. This only supports my mind set that Heidi's case isn't cold, it's open and active.

Although Heidi remains missing, the dedication to find her and everyone involved in her kidnapping is kept at the forefront of the sheriff's department case load. A fact many don't know, even those locally, is that the Oswego County Sheriff has had new hires and new investigators review Heidi's case to see if anything was missed. Sheriff Todd, Heidi's lead investigator, and the DA keep in close contact with the family. They are open and honest with us and leave the communication paths continually open, even offering their private numbers in case we need to call. I understand this is rare in complex cases, especially in what most deem a cold case. After twenty-five years, they still call or stop by the house to check on us and update us as tips, leads, and other information are available.

Let me move off my soap box of why my sister's case is not cold, and introduce you to my sister the person, as opposed to the missing person and missing child's poster most associate her with.

During Heidi's junior year of high school, the school, Bishop Cunningham Junior/Senior High School, had to close their doors due to financial burden. Heidi had a choice to make: return to her home district, Mexico Academy and Central Schools, or apply for college a year early. Her determination to reach her goals motivated her to choose the latter. She was accepted at Onondaga Community College and completed her last year of high school and first year of college simultaneously with honors.

Heidi's determination helped her face the adversity of being one of the youngest college freshmen on campus, to work full time, and still find time to have a social life. She was on target to graduate in May 1994, yet this had denied her. The college invited my parents to attend graduation and receive Heidi's degree certificate because they stated Heidi's grades were such that she could have scored a zero on her final grades and still graduated with honors. As if this wasn't a blessing, the college refunded Heidi's tuition for the semester to offset the expense of running the Heidi Allen Command Center. The Onondaga Community College's dedication to its students isn't just in their mission statement, it's in their actions. To my knowledge, this is still true today.

As I look back, so much has changed since 1994. At the time of Heidi's kidnapping, the National Center for Missing & Exploited Children (NCMEC) couldn't help us with the search efforts for Heidi because she was eighteen. It wasn't until 2006, when Suzanne's Law passed, that Heidi was included in the database. Suzanne's Law makes sure all missing children, including those in college, and their families have the same opportunity for maximum support during the early and most valuable moments after a child's disappearance. More important, this law is responsible for activating law enforcement immediately when a child in college goes missing.

For more information, visit definitions.uslegal.com/s/suzannes-law/. A special thanks to Suzanne's parents, Doug and Mary Lyall, for their years of dedication to make this a reality. It's because of this law that Heidi and others were added to the NCMEC database.

Although we didn't have the support of NCMEC, we had the help of Sara Anne Wood's family. Sara disappeared the prior year. After her disappearance, their command center transitioned into a poster distribution center for the National Center for Missing & Exploited Children. Their help with posters and setting up our command center were priceless. Our small community rallied to form a unified and Heidi-driven team.

After two days and no sleep, everyone doing all they knew to do, and the help from Sara Anne Wood's family, we still needed help. A search and rescue expert from San Antonio was brought in. My aunt did a Google search, and found the Heidi Search Center. They were a nonprofit dedicated to training people and then sending them across the country to help families find their missing children. The search expert, Rick, brought both expertise and hope to our tired and sad community. An answered prayer.

The next few months were a blur, lost in the stages of grief. I took a leave of absence because I didn't want to leave the command center—if Heidi were to be found, I didn't want her to think I had moved on.

The following year, my husband Ed insisted we get away for the weekend. I didn't want to go, but my parent's insisted, so I agreed. It's important to remember we didn't have cellphones in our pockets and purses in the early 90s. My parents loaned us their big cellular phone so they could call us in case we needed to return home. I wasn't sure about leaving, but everyone insisted it was needed and was best. I only agreed because my parents promised to call if Heidi was found or if anything new happened.

We went to Canada's Wonderland for one day, enjoyed a restful night's sleep, then had breakfast the next morning before checking out and returning home. It felt as if a weight was lifted and like it might be possible to be human again, but this feeling didn't last long.

Upon returning to our hotel room after breakfast, the red light on the phone flashed, indicating we had a message at the front desk. I called the desk but the line was busy, so I took the stairs to the lobby while my husband grabbed our luggage and met me there. I put change into the payphone and dialed my parents' home number. A stranger answered the phone. I asked to speak to my mom and was told, "I can take a message. The family isn't receiving phone calls at this time."

I'd like to say I was calm and kind in my response, but frustration and anxiety ruled my mind and tongue. "This is Lisa, and I want to speak to my mother. She called me and I'm not hanging up until I talk to her," I demanded.

I could hear whispering and within a few moments my mom was on the other end of the phone.

"Lisa, it's okay. We haven't found Heidi. Take a deep breath. Lisa?"

I couldn't speak. Next thing I knew, my husband, Ed, pried the phone from my fingers and talked with my mom. I slid down the wall and cried. I didn't know what happened or what my mom was telling Ed, but I knew it couldn't be good. I heard him tell Mom we'd be leaving once we checked out and, "She'll be okay, I've got her."

After hanging up the phone, he knelt down, looked me square in the eyes and said, "There was a break in the case, an arrest. Your parents weren't going to call, but it was in the local newspaper and they were afraid we'd see it in a newspaper if we stopped for gas, so they called. I told her we'd leave. Lisa? Do you hear me? Lisa?"

The rest is a blur. One thing I'm sure of is that a supportive husband is a priceless gem. I remember stopping at EVERY gas station and rest area looking for a newspaper to tell me more.

My parents weren't specific, just that there was a break in the case and two arrests were made. We didn't know who, all we knew was that it was time to get home and wouldn't be stopping at Niagara Falls as planned. Instead, the trauma and stress made the trip home feel more like a flight than a ride. Once we arrived in my parents' driveway, I learned two brothers had been arrested.

I did not leave town again for years, out of fear something would happen if I left. This wasn't rational, but it was how I felt. I've since learned that this is normal for families of the missing. Life is forever changed as we wait for the phone to ring with news of a recovery. Then, as days turn to weeks, months, and years, we wait for news of more likely a discovery instead of recovery.

To leave town and vacation still triggers much anxiety within me, but I know if I'm to heal and move forward, I must face my fears, overcome the anxiety and take a vacation now and again. It's healing.

I don't know about you, but after the loss of a loved one, a person goes into survival mode. The way I survived was staying close to home—it was another ten or so years before I left town. Twenty-five years later, it's easier to travel with new technologies, too. We didn't have phones in our pockets, live news or live updates in the early nineties.

I've shared how challenging it was for me to leave town. It was also very difficult to work. I struggled to put my feet on the floor and face other people. The original plan was to work, and my mom would update me on my lunch break, but I was so distracted and emotional, a family leave became necessary. My employer was understanding and offered as much time as I needed.

Arrests led to hearings and court cases. I went from being useless at work to a warm body sitting in the courtroom but at least I was with my parents, family, and friends. In a sense, I was hearing everything first-hand but at the end of the day, I couldn't tell you what I heard or who I even sat next to. Two-plus decades later, the fog is covered with cobwebs. I used to beat myself up for not remembering, but today I understand this is part of the process and is normal.

Two brothers were charged and tried for the kidnapping and presumption of death of my sister, Heidi Allen. They were tried separately, the first acquitted and the second convicted from twenty-five years to life in prison. In 2018, the convicted brother, Gary Thibodeau, died in prison without ever revealing Heidi's location.

Each member of the family, Heidi's friends, and even community members responded to and handled the loss differently. There isn't a right and wrong way to grieve after such a tragic loss. Homicide and cold cases leave a different impact on one's life than remembering a loved one ten or twenty years after their death. If you remember nothing else from my writing, remember this: it's normal and okay to accept, grieve, and move forward in different ways than those around you. The key is to be moving forward and not lying in bed all the time.

Over the past twenty-five years, there have been too many calls, breaking news stories, and tips to recall them all. Yet, each still had the power to take me back to 1994.

After the twentieth anniversary of Heidi's kidnapping, a defense attorney took it upon herself to follow what she called new leads in the case. She and a local reporter worked together without input or support of Heidi's family to follow up on these supposed leads, but left law enforcement and the district attorney out of the investigation.

The first we heard about this investigation was in July 2014, when a young reporter showed up at my parents' home. She shared information about the defense attorney and investigative reporter's findings, and wanted a statement. We refused, to which the reporter informed us that it didn't matter if we gave a statement or not—an article would go live within minutes anyway. My parents were so upset, they nearly fell and needed to sit down. The naïve reporter ignored my parents leaning against the house, and asked if she could take a picture. She was told that no pictures would be taken, and told to leave and never return to our private property again. She appeared dumbfounded and couldn't understand our reactions. The veteran cameraman, on the other hand, was already retreating to the car and shaking his head at her naivety.

This media outlet said they gave us a chance to respond, even though they spent months sneaking around and plotting to visit us.

Mom called the sheriff, but before we could contact family, the live news was breaking on the internet and family was calling us. Of course, we had no information for them because we only knew what the young reporter told us.

To make matters worse, the Sheriff's Department and district attorney were unaware of the investigation. It is moments like this that give us a bitter taste of the media. Not all media agencies function like this, but sadly it only takes one to ruin it for everyone. This is just one example of how the media impacts, controls, destroys, and abuses the victim, and revictimizes families for the sake of a story and ratings.

To be fair, most media waited to contact us, letting this one news outlet run their story and updates every hour. As this developed from speculation to an actual law enforcement investigation, everyone was involved and reaching out to the family.

Prior to 2014, my parents handled all the press conferences and press. Due to health concerns, I stepped up and became my parents' voice. There was a potential discovery site and the media were all camped out there, so rather than respond to each one independently, my parents and I drafted a response. My aunt drove me over and I read the statement. If it hadn't been written down, I probably would have only stood there and cried, with my emotions getting the best of me. By doing it this way, my parents' message was given in the words they would have spoken.

The general public posted negative comments about me reading from a script, and this bothered me. Thankfully, wonderful friends reminded me that the words I read were put together with my parents to encourage and give hope to the community. I couldn't let the criticism of a few take that away. Friends are another gem one needs when your loved one is known as a cold case more than a person.

Over the next few years there were multiple hearings, countless articles, news stories, press conferences, interviews with Dateline and Investigation Discovery with Tamron Hall, meetings with the sheriff, the sheriff investigators, the district attorney, and the ADA.

My parents are retired, and the stress took a toll on their health. The final New York State appeal was only denied in spring of 2018, four years after this chaotic part of the journey began.

In September 2015, my mother died from cancer on my sister's birthday. The stress induced by one news agency's tactics crushed my mother's spirit and increased the decline of her health. With each new article, phone call, or headline, my mother's hope transitioned into a deeper despair.

My father, watching his wife struggle, stepped back to be primary caregiver, leaving me to step up as lead in Heidi's case and media contacts. I was not ready but then again, one is never ready for this. It is a role we must do, not one chosen. I was, and am, honored to be able to do this for my parents and Heidi. It's not easy and I make mistakes. I let my emotions show far too often. This is where I have positives to share about the media. As I sat in one of the court hearings listening to one of the people on the stand detail how they think my sister was murdered, I thought I'd pass out. Mind you, I thought I had a poker face until I received a text from one of the reporters, "Relax your cheeks, take a deep breath. They are scanning the camera to you." I was grateful and did as she suggested.

These moments are real and still vivid. One thing I've learned is that some things are so solid and clear while others are foggy and gray. I think this is the effect of stress on our bodies. Living life on the edge of not knowing and wondering takes a toll on one's health, well-being, and faith.

Faith is where I had the most transformation. I saved this for the end because I like to end my presentations and messages on a positive note and one of hope.

Life can be overwhelming and feel unbearable when one doesn't have something to believe in. My belief lies in God, and a relationship with Jesus Christ. I give thanks to one of my students, who saw what

I needed and had the child-like faith and courage to invite me. His kindness, honesty, and concern brought me to church, and God did the rest.

Despite the many ups and downs, I'm thankful for all I have experienced. There isn't a day when I don't wish my sister was still here. There isn't a time when I don't wish she was spoiling her niece and we were still spending Thursdays, sister day, together with each other and with our kids. But this isn't the reality God chose for me.

The reality I have is to hold out hope for Heidi's return, and to encourage, inspire, and help others grieving the loss of a loved one to know they can and will survive. It won't be easy, it doesn't happen in a straight line, but it will happen. One day, one foot, and one memory at a time until all the questions have been answered. It might not be in our lifetime, but if we mentor the next generation, our loved ones will never be forgotten. We have the power, control, and ability to keep their names, stories, memories, and cases in the forefront until they are solved.

LISA M. BUSKE, Heidi's sister

CHAPTER TWENTY-ONE

DeColbie J. Esco

BY DIANA PIERCE
Coby's mom

On August 24, 2012, my thirty-year-old son DeColbie (Coby) J. Esco Sr. and I went to downtown Chicago to file for joint custody of his son. It was something we had discussed for some time. After filing the necessary paperwork, we decided to stay and window shop.

We were in and out of stores, and at one point we separated because I wanted to go into a different store. Coby's friend worked downtown, and they met up on his lunch break. Coby and I decided to meet later at Urban Outfitters.

Coby graduated from Wingate University and went to work for One Hope United in their child development center. One of the moments I remember about that day is the conversation we had while heading downtown. I thought Coby would do what he always did while riding in a car or train: sleep. However, on this day he didn't and instead became very talkative. He went on and on about his students at One Hope United, and talked about how smart and funny they were. He was very fond of them.

We also talked about a shoe ad he had seen in a store window. When he asked me what I thought, I said, "You can't go wrong with buying one pair and getting a second pair for a dollar. If you don't like them, you can always give them away."

Coby was very good at giving. About a week before his murder, he cleared out his closet and gave away two large bags of clothing. Anyway, Coby had decided to buy those shoes and was wearing them the night of his murder as he ran for his life.

As I further reflect on that day, it was so beautiful—sunny and pleasant. When we returned from downtown, Colby asked me to cook him a rice and fish dish. Before my feet could hit the floor, he decided to prepare the rice himself. That was a first. Maybe it was because I had worked overnight and he wanted to give me a break. Whatever the reason, I appreciated it.

With Coby taking charge of his meal I went to bed. Later, he appeared in my bedroom doorway and said he was going out to meet up with some of his friends. He proudly pointed to his new shoes, and then closed the door. He opened it again seconds later and said, "By the way, all we had was brown rice and I don't like brown rice." Those were the last words he ever spoke to me.

After he left, I tried to go back to sleep but the air conditioner wasn't working right, and I was having trouble catching my breath. I finally got the air conditioner adjusted and dozed off.

I woke up around 2:45 a.m. and noticed several missed calls on my phone. One of them said Coby had been hurt and was in the hospital. When I first listened to that message, I thought Coby probably had a broken arm or leg, I would nurse him back to health, and all would be well. Then a feeling of dread overcame me, and I feared that wouldn't be the case.

When I arrived at the hospital, I was told Coby had died at 2:53 a.m. A doctor began to tell me everything that had happened to my son's body, but I was numb and wasn't getting it. In my dazed mind, Coby had simply been involved in some sort of accident. Then the news began to penetrate.

Coby had been violently and deliberately attacked. He and some friends had left a barbershop around 10:30 p.m. and boarded the Western Avenue bus southbound to the Brown Line. After getting off the bus at Foster Avenue, Coby and his friends were approached by an individual who asked them, "Who do you represent?"

I was told Coby walked away from this person as a van pulled up and stopped. Several guys jumped out and there was a fight, but it quickly broke up. Coby and his friends then continued walking toward the Brown Line as more vehicles showed up and chased them down. One of the vehicles hit Coby, dragged him for two blocks, and ran over him multiple times. His broken body was left on the street like trash.

Coby's murder took my breath away. It has consumed me. All I can think about is getting justice for him, and helping others in similar situations fight for their own justice.

When I think about law enforcement, I actually get physically ill. Maybe I watched too many shows like Law & Order. Maybe I expected too much. Anyway, no one from the police called or came to see me. I called them to see if they had made an arrest, and they had not.

After Coby was laid to rest, I called the police again. Amazingly, they didn't even know who DeColbie Esco was. He was simply a number attached to a hit-and-run incident, not a homicide. They tried to convince me this was in fact a hit-and-run accident. They were very short, cold, and uncooperative. Whenever I called, it seemed like the investigator was never available. I believe in my heart that law enforcement did not do the very best job they could have—far from it.

My dealings with the district attorney's office were also cold and lacked compassion. Their attitude was stunning to me. I was always at a loss for words when speaking with anyone in authority about Coby's case. I had the impression they didn't care, which made me very angry. However, that anger strengthened my resolve to fight.

I was also disappointed in the news media. The few articles that were written about Coby's death weren't accurate for the most part. They never called me or knocked on my door to learn the real story. I believe that because Coby wasn't gunned down, the story of his death wasn't exciting enough to warrant attention. I even called television and radio stations, but none showed any interest in doing more.

In looking back, the first few weeks after the murder are a blur. The only thing I clearly recall is my desperate need for the truth, trying to find out what happened to my son. I was referred from one police station to another. I was being led around like a puppy and felt as though I was moving like a robot.

Three weeks later, I drove to the scene of the crime. I regretted not having gone there the first day. I wasn't coping with Coby's death very well.

Around that same time, I returned to work. I believe getting back to my job helped keep me sane. It wasn't easy, but it was better than being alone. My coworkers were kind and gentle, but not supportive regarding my efforts to get justice for Coby and bring awareness to his murder—they didn't want to get involved.

At first, when people asked me about Coby's death, it was very difficult to respond—I would simply cry. Eventually I was able to say, "He was murdered."

Now, after the passage of time, I answer without hesitation, "My son was murdered."

Will anyone ever be held accountable for Coby's death? I don't know the answer to that. All I do know for sure is that I will never give up my quest for answers and justice.

DIANA PIERCE, Coby's mom

We are demanding police transparency and
accountability so we can build trust and work
together to make our communities safer.

-MALCOLM JENKINS

CHAPTER TWENTY-TWO

Holly K. Piirainen

BY CARLA M. JACKMAN
Holly's aunt

It was during a string of hazy, hot and humid days in August 1993, when our family experienced the worst tragedy imaginable.

My brother Rick decided to use his vacation days. He took his three kids to my parents' summer home, the Camp, on South Pond in Sturbridge, Massachusetts, for a week of boating, fishing and fun.

Ten-year old Holly, Rick's oldest, called me the night of August 4, to ask if I and my kids could come visit the next day. Unfortunately, I declined as I was preparing for a weekend away. That night was the last time I spoke with Holly. I've often thought that if I had said yes to Holly's request, maybe the following would never have happened.

Sometime around noon on Thursday, August 5, 1993, Holly and her five-year-old brother Zach walked up South Shore Drive to visit a new litter of puppies they had seen the night before. Not long after, Zach returned alone. Rick asked where Holly was, and Zach said she was still waiting for the puppies to come out.

Rick sent his middle child, eight-year-old Andy, up the road to fetch his sister. Andy returned without Holly and was holding one of Holly's sneakers he found on the side of the road. Rick immediately jumped in his Jeep and drove to where Andy found the sneaker. Fearing the worst, he drove up and down South Shore Drive hoping for some sign of his daughter. Failing to find her, panic set it and he rushed back to the Camp to call the police.

Someone had snatched the beautiful, blonde-haired, brown-eyed, innocent Holly! She was gone in an instant. No one heard her scream, no one heard a car peel out, no one saw her abduction. Our lives changed forever from that moment on.

My husband and I raced to the Camp. When we reached Allen Road, we came upon the police command stationed at the corner of Allen Road and South Shore Drive, where Holly was last known to have been. Search dogs were brought in and helicopters soon appeared overhead. There were ground, air, and water searches. Hundreds of people volunteered to search by foot, and some friends searched on ATVs. This lasted for days. I'll never forget the feeling of seeing the helicopter flying overhead. Tears rolled down my cheeks, my stomach felt nauseous. The shock, horror and helplessness began to set in.

The police quickly realized this was not a runaway case. This was an abduction. Holly was not a troubled child, she was not from the Sturbridge area, but from Grafton. She was on vacation and there was no set routine. She wouldn't wander off with only one shoe on. She was a responsible young girl who had been taught stranger danger.

We felt so helpless. Rick was told not to leave the Camp as his scent could throw off the dogs. We were terrified, we cried, and we prayed. We asked the police questions: How long can she survive without food and water? Who could have done this? What can we do?

We were told the first forty-eight hours are crucial. That forty-eight hours came and went. We would send the little kids (Holly's brothers and four cousins) downstairs to the family room when our discussions got too scary for them to hear.

On the first or second day, an officer told us it was better if we didn't talk to the media. We couldn't fathom not pleading to the public for help, so we did just that. We also talked to anyone who would offer their help or their services. Posters were produced. A friend arranged to have a billboard put up. We searched on our own in pairs, we hung posters, and prayed. Holly's mom and I sat on the side of the road for hours taking down license plate numbers of passing cars. The police told us that if we knew who some of our summer neighbors were, we would not have let our kids out of the house—there was a heavy population of sexual offenders in the local area. We didn't know.

The police told us to keep a log of any tips, any information given to us. While leads poured into the police station, the Camp phone was ringing. Most were friends and family, of course, but some were locals trying to report who they thought could have done this, and psychics who wanted to share their theories. We listened to them all. We took turns writing down information with the promise that police would come every week to review everything we wrote down, a promise that was not entirely carried out.

We felt alone in our panic, trapped in this living nightmare. Our family and friends came with food and prayers for us, but there was not really a liaison between us and the police.

The summer drew to a close. Days went by without any news. We felt like zombies, just going through the motions of daily living, yet feeling so frantic inside. How could the rest of the world go on like nothing has happened while we were in such incredible pain? We had to try to keep life as normal as we could for Rick's two boys and the young cousins who, in their innocence, had believed the world was a safe place—an innocence that is now gone.

In the first few days, a local man offered to host a vigil. We did not judge this person, and humbly accepted his offer. We sat outside a school in the neighboring town, looking pretty desperate, I'm sure. People came by and offered their condolences and dropped money in a bucket to help us with whatever we needed. This person also ran a few other benefits to raise money. I'm not at liberty to share his name, since soon after Holly's body was found he was named a person of interest, among many others. I'm not at liberty to share the names of the others, either, but believe they all know who they are. Here we are, twenty-five years later, still waiting to find out who among them is the one responsible for killing our Holly.

The day finally came when the beginning chapter closed and the next one opened. That day will be etched in my mind forever. On October 23, 1993, the first day of hunting season, three hunters found the remains of Holly in a shallow grave covered with leaves and branches. My brother was the first to hear, and rushed to the scene but wasn't allowed to go to his daughter's remains.

When I found out, I remember asking the police if they were sure. Yes, her sneaker was found at the scene. I remember asking if we could see her one more time, and being told no. Animals had gotten to her. I remember the sobbing and the heart-wrenching sadness.

I'm unable to give much detail of the cause of her death, but as you can imagine, it was not pleasant. Even at only ten years old, we knew Holly had put up a good fight.

Telling our youngest family members what happened were the most difficult conversations we've ever had. We had held on to hope that maybe someone took Holly and would return her, or that we would finally find her, but this was not the case. Again, horror, fear and realization set in. How could we assure our children they would be safe ever again?

On November 13, 1993, Holly's remains were laid to rest in her hometown of Grafton. Attendance at both the wake and funeral were enormous. The media was there. The police videotaped both events with hopes of possibly capturing the image or behavior of possible suspects. One of the suspects did attend, although he had changed his appearance. Later the police informed us the videotape was lost. We never saw it.

Worcester County turned Holly's case over to Hampden County DA's office because the location where her body was found crossed over from Worcester to Hampden. We feared information was not being fully shared between them, and suspected that evidence may not have been handled properly, or even worse, lost completely.

We never received a copy of the autopsy report but were told of its general findings. Some of the facts police told us about the scene where Holly was found were later found to be misinformation relayed to us by previous officers on the case.

Early on, Carl Westerman, a private investigator, offered his services pro bono. We accepted his offer and poured our hearts out to him. He worked hard coming up with a theory, but it didn't pan out. I don't remember if the police were very cooperative with him back then. I know the police were overwhelmed by the number of leads coming in, and had to prioritize which leads to follow first.

There have been at least half dozen strong suspects or persons of interest over the years. Two weeks after Holly's abduction, twelve-year-old Sara Wood was out for a bike ride in upstate New York when she went missing. We thought it may be the same person who took Holly, but it didn't pan out. A man named Lewis Lent later confessed to killing Sara when he was caught trying to abduct another girl.

Over the years, detectives on Holly's case have changed. Most who worked on the case cannot shake it from their minds. There's a group of suspects who were acquaintances, some of whom have since passed. There are a few loners on the radar that may never crack, since they obviously have no conscience.

Every anniversary, we've met with the police and they have tried to tell us as much as they can without jeopardizing the case. Every year we are asked to be patient and wait for DNA technology to get more advanced. Every year we get the same questions from the media: "Tell us what happened. How did it make you feel? Are you still hopeful the case will be solved? What kind of little girl was Holly?"

Last year, 2018, was a big anniversary for us—twenty-five years. It hit harder than expected, maybe because there was so much more media coverage. We planned a vigil and had a billboard up around the state, and new reward posters were created.

This year our hopes were renewed when we learned that Colonel Kerry Gilpin was appointed Superintendent of the Massachusetts State Police. We found out that she, too, had a family member who was abducted and murdered. Finally, we had someone at the top who knows exactly how we feel. We got to meet with Colonel Gilpin and with Springfield's district attorney, Anthony Gulluni, who both assured us that Holly's case is one of their top priorities. We also have a renewed hope with the advances in DNA technology.

We also had the good fortune of meeting a cold case consultant, Dr. Sarah Stein, from The Center of Resolution of Unresolved Crime in 2017. Pro bono, we were able to get sound advice and felt more prepared to meet with the police. Dr. Stein freely shared with us and the police what her own research uncovered. Dr. Stein may not have had full cooperation with the police, but we feel having her on our side gave us strength. She helped us organize a vigil this past October. Several people called the tip line, and some stopped by in person to give us information.

The police have strongly advised us not to share information freely with our cold case consultant, Dr. Stein, as it could jeopardize Holly's case, which is something we certainly don't want to do. We feel torn. We have expressed to the police our feeling of not being supported by an advocate over the years, and have been recently promised that this will change. We are cautiously optimistic that things will move forward with Holly's case, and renewed support from the police has been encouraging.

Over the years, our family has had its share of struggles dealing with Holly's abduction and murder. To this day, some of us live with posttraumatic stress disorder, high anxiety and fear, horrible night-mares, and struggle with addiction. Still we persevere. People say we are strong and, "I don't know how you do it," to which we respond, "We have no choice."

We appreciate the empathy, but we really feel understood by others who have suffered this same type of horrific loss. Now having Colonel Gilipin at the helm gives us more hope that everyone is giving it their best effort to solve Holly's case.

There is no handbook to tell family and friends of a homicide victim what to expect— if only there was. If I were to write this type of a handbook, one of the first things on my checklist would be to demand for a well-qualified police advocate immediately assigned to help families and to stay in touch. Another would be to make sure the police get fingerprints from your child's belongings right away.

If your child is missing, there is an organization I admire and might consider joining some day called Team HOPE. All the members must have had, or still have, a missing loved one.

A few authors have asked if we would share Holly's story. It has been covered by newspapers, TV news, talk shows, crime shows, and most recently a podcast. The Justice for Holly Piirainen Facebook page was created by our family.

After a recent meeting with the police and our Springfield-based police advocate, we learned about a homicide program in Springfield that helps support struggling family members. If only we had known about this sooner. We're currently looking in Worcester County to see if we can find a similar program.

We have a better relationship with the police nowadays, and hold out hope that Holly's murder will be solved. It was not my intent to relay the impression that the police are not doing everything they can now, but to briefly fill the reader in on what has gone on since Holly's murder.

Holly should still be with us today. Someone needs to be accountable. We will hold her in our hearts forever and pray for justice. Holly deserves it.

CARLA M. JACKMAN, Holly's aunt

POLICE INFORMATION FOR TIPS:
Text a tip to: CRIMES or 274637 subject line: Solve Holly Piirainen
Email: thomas.w.sullivan3@massmail.state.ma.us.
Telephone: 413-505-5993.
Family-run Facebook page: Justice for Holly Piirainen:
Facebook.com/hollypiirainen

CHAPTER TWENTY-THREE

Alonzo Thomas, IV

BY MONIQUE WILLIS
Alonzo's mom

Life and death change things. Your world changes when you birth a child and bring them into the world, and things change when you bury them. You are not supposed to bury your child. They are supposed to bury you. When your child's death  occurs from senseless gun violence, and not from a health issue or a freak accident, you will have more questions—who, what, why, and sometimes when.

On May 28, 1993, Alonzo Thomas IV was born, and on April 5, 2014, he was taken from us. He was murdered. He was with familiar people, some of whom he referred to as friends.

The story goes that he was on the phone, possibly talking to the person who took his life, giving them directions to where he was.

Alonzo was visiting a home on 71st and Wayne in Kansas City. He grew up in this neighborhood and was very familiar with his surroundings. When the person arrived, the story gets a little shaky. Was the number of people in the vehicle two or three? Was Alonzo in the car or outside the car? Was there an argument or fight? Did some of them get out of the car and run? What did Alonzo do to them that warranted him being shot? The only answer that I know for sure is, my only child was murdered, and I needed to start planning a funeral and figure out what happened to him.

In order to start the process, I needed to know where my son's body was, and called the medical examiner's office looking for him. They confirmed that they had him, but I couldn't see him until he was released to a funeral home. How do you plan to make arrangements for a funeral when you have not seen the body?

My only understanding of this process is what I've seen on TV. I should've been able to identify Alonzo's body at the medical examiner's office, but TV does not equal reality. He did have his ID on him, which confirmed his identity. I have a cousin who works for a funeral home and I called her for some guidance. She instructed me to select a funeral home, and then I would be able to see Alonzo.

I remember having a houseful of people. I designated a friend to take over the house while I left with my mother, cousin, and another friend, to view Alonzo's body.

He was lying on the table as though sleeping peacefully. It was a very calming experience. I'm not sure why or how, but it gave me peace to see him. I asked to see his whole body but he was naked and with the autopsy scars, I was advised not to look.

Alonzo's funeral was held on Friday, April 11, 2014. I recall making the arrangements at the funeral home with my mother, sister, and cousin. My mother picked out the headstone that was probably made for a toddler because of the duck images, but she insisted that was the right one because Alonzo loved animals. I picked out a blue casket because that was his favorite color. I had insurance, my family worked at the funeral home and owned the cemetery, so there was no financial burden. I felt as if I was being taken care of, and not taken advantage of.

Finalizing the paperwork and signing on the dotted line was an emotional overload—knowing I had just paid for my son's funeral seemed surreal to me. I felt as if I was being taken care of and not being taken advantage of. After signing, I was ready to leave, no more conversation. On the way home, I sat in the backseat and tears rolled down my face, as they did when I first heard about my son being shot.

When I arrived home, the media were parked in front of my house and a business card was stuck in the door. I thought them being there was disrespectful. They were looking for a story, trying to catch a grieving mother being distraught. Their services could have been better used as investigative reporters looking into Alonzo's murder. My cousin asked them to leave.

Family and friends were in and out of my house from April 5 to April 11. The day of the funeral, no one was allowed to come in and hang out as they had been doing all week. I wanted peace and quiet. When the funeral home's limousines pulled up, I came outside and my family was waiting on me. We prayed in a circle in front of my home and then left for the church.

Alonzo's daycare teacher and family friend spoke at his funeral. Her words have been the most helpful to me during my grieving process. She spoke on "My Little Lamb," ALONZO THOMAS IV. Romans 8:28 declares, "And we know that ALL things work together for good to them that love God, to them who are then called according to HIS purpose."

When you think of that Scripture, especially during this time when you have the extremely difficult task of laying your loved one—your only begotten son—you have to lay him to rest! So, Monique, perhaps you say that "Romans 8:28 surely can't apply to my situation right now." Alonzo Thomas IV started out being and will forever be a little lamb.

In this devastating situation, Alonzo became somewhat of a sacrificial lamb. Mind you, he is not THE sacrificial lamb! However, I want you to know this is what the Lord has spoken.

"Because of this sacrifice, folks who knew and loved Alonzo Thomas IV are going to come to believe AND THEN KNOW that ALL things do work together for good. And because ALL things work together for good and for God's divine purpose for our lives . . . because of this little lamb . . . God gave His only begotten Son . . . to die that we might live! This little lamb . . . his life was taken; literally snatched from us all. . . and it is still that someone here might be able to live! So, while we may ask how any good thing can come out of this, mark my words, watch and see! Lives are going to be forever changed today . . . and it will all be because of God's love for us . . . and because of the life of this little lamb!" ~Pastor Cassandra Wainright

I returned to work on April 21, 2014. I thought I was ready—I thought going back to work would make my life feel normal. I was wrong. I was not ready. I would suggest to anyone in that position to wait. Take time off for as long as you can financially afford to.

Thankfully, my supervisor at that time was very understanding and accommodating. There were times when I would disappear and text her, saying that I was having a bad moment as I sat in my car and cried. Sometimes I would come back inside and go back to work. And there were a few times when I would come in, get my stuff, and tell her I had to leave for the day. One of those days was when the funeral home called and told me that Alonzo's death certificate was ready.

Knowing that Alonzo had a death certificate was an unsettling final moment, confirming that this nightmare was real. It brought home the fact that something in my life and in my heart had changed forever, and there was a point of no return.

Alonzo's daughter, Zoey, was about two years old at the time. Whenever she saw flowers, she would want to take them to her daddy. I hadn't ordered a vase for Alonzo's grave because I knew I wouldn't use it. Months later, I called the funeral home and ordered one so Zoey would have a place to put her daddy's flowers.

My house is empty. Everyone, including Alonzo, is gone. I have his case number—14-22567—but his murder remains unsolved.

On April 7, an organization came to my house to inform me about Crime Victims Compensation. I met with a victim advocate on April 14, completed my CVC paperwork and learned who my detective was.

On April 15, the detective came to see me. He had Alonzo's phone, which was still locked. I had one of Alonzo's friends come over to unlock the phone for him. Ten days had gone by—wasted. I felt the phone should have been unlocked much sooner, and it would have been had the police contacted me, but they hadn't. There was no communication between us that could have led to accessing the possibly vital information that might have been in the phone that may have led to an arrest.

On April 21, members of the Kansas City Police Department and I canvassed the neighborhood with reward flyers. Community leaders and I handed out flyers on June 13, at Gregory and Prospect. We distributed more flyers at surrounding locations on June 28, and July 19. On August 28, I was on the front page of the Kansas City Star because of my efforts to find out who murdered my son. The article was titled, "Grieving mother finds her mission."

On September 9, Kansas City Crime Stoppers sent out a press release offering a four-thousand-dollar reward. On September 12, The Call newspaper ran Alonzo's reward flyer. On September 22, Lamar Advertising put up a billboard for Alonzo's reward.

On October 28, I presented to the Kansas City Board of Police Commissioners with questions about their lack of communication, and that I needed to make sure they were aware of Alonzo and his case being unsolved. A deputy chief pulled me aside and promised better communication. Three other officers also told me they were aware of the communication issues and were trying to put together a task force. I never heard from the three officers again, and the deputy chief later transferred out of the department

A KCT-5 newsperson spoke to me and aired my story that same day. I was able to record the news story and post it to YouTube at Youtube.com/watch?v=PA1WEczZ0E4. The entire meeting was recorded, and I was able to get a copy of that as well. I have yet to be able to sit down and review it because it was such an overwhelming and emotional moment. I can't even remember anything I said. The whole situation is frustrating, irritating, and surreal.

As you can see, my personal experience with law enforcement has not been ideal. I was out of town when Alonzo was murdered. I arrived late in the evening trying to make contact with people who had been engaged with the police department. The numbers they gave me led to voicemails, and I left messages. No one seemed to be concerned or helpful.

I understand the case is open and that police need to keep some information confidential, but they need to understand and respect that families need answers. There are many holes and gaps in their communication process. Every detail imaginable (without hindering the case) should have been provided to a mother who has lost her only child. I know their job is hard. Still, I would like for them to respect the needs of the families, and respond to them accordingly. I would like proof that they are actively and professionally working on solving the case. I think that Alonzo's file is sitting under a stack of paperwork somewhere.

Alonzo's original detective was transferred elsewhere, and I only learned of it when I attempted to contact him. When I questioned why I wasn't informed, they couldn't tell me. Last I heard, a sergeant is now the lead investigator.

Alonzo's homicide made breaking news with at least three major news stations (some links may have been removed and archived):

- http://fox4kc.com/2014/04/05/police-search-for-shooting-suspect-who-fled-scene-on-foot/
- http://www.kshb.com/news/crime/one-dead-after-kcmo-shooting
- http://www.kctv5.com/story/25171635/police-investigate-deadly-shooting-in-kcmo-neighborhood

I now have to contact the media so they can bring some light to Alonzo's unsolved homicide. When I notify them, I hope they will cooperate and share my story. Unfortunately, if they feel another story is more important, I know his story will be swept under the rug. The media seem to participate more when it's a different kind of tragedy, such as police brutality against a black person, or if the murder victim is an infant or a very young child. Trying to get their attention when

I want to talk about the investigation or announce a fundraising event to benefit Momma On a Mission, Inc., is hard to do. They spotlight things that, to me, don't appear newsworthy. And stories that tend to go viral on social media are usually something stupid.

I want to talk a little bit about what Alonzo's murder did to me emotionally, and how it impacted my relationships with others.

I fell into a deep depression. I don't think the people around me knew or fully understood what was going on with me. I tend to be withdrawn, so people think I am mean or distant. You would think that family and friends who know you, and know your only child has been murdered, would understand that a major change has occurred in your life and things are different. I was trying to figure out and find my new normal. When I got upset, I got really upset and emotional. I've been fortunate to have been able to remove myself from those situations before erupting and saying or doing something I might regret.

When sad and depressed, I was unable to shake my emotions. I used a close friend as my therapist. I also pursued an official licensed therapist. My first two therapists helped me pro bono because of my circumstance. I can honestly say that I got what I paid for—nothing. The first therapist sought me out because of my story in the Kansas City Star. She was very informative on the business end when I shared that I wanted to start my own nonprofit organization, and provided a lot of details and resources. However, she fell short on the therapist end, and with her follow-through on resources and phone calls.

I found the second therapist through a local organization that provide services to families of homicide victims. She kept asking me the same questions over and over again. I told her I was depressed, and she even said that I looked depressed. I told her that I was having a hard time concentrating and focusing on my duties while at work. I provided the same answer, and after repeating myself so many times, I shut down and knew she was not the one for me. Afterwards she mentioned that we could have coffee and hang out together if I needed someone to talk to. I told her I would call her if needed, knowing that I probably never would. She did suggest that I see a psychiatrist, and I took her up on her advice.

I had insurance through my employer, so I was able to find someone and give them a copay for their services. After my first appointment with the psychiatrist, I walked out with prescriptions for depression, ADD, insomnia and anxiety. He also referred me to a psychologist in his office. The paid psychologist was not that helpful to me, so I stopped seeing him and continued to use my friend as my therapist. However, I continued seeing the psychiatrist until one day I asked him what would happen if I stopped taking the medicines. He told me to stop and see. So, I did. I found I still needed medication to help with my insomnia, and occasionally need something to help me focus. I have occasional bouts of anxiety and depression, but I am no longer using any of those medicines.

Although the psychologist told me to try to be around people more because isolation is not helpful, I cope with my mental health by isolating myself and avoiding people. It helps when dodging the dreaded question, "How are you doing?" I understand that people mean well, but I feel that no one really wants to know how I am doing or can help me feel better.

Grief. Everyone grieves differently. Don't let anyone tell you how to grieve or when to grieve. The nerve of some people who think that you should be over it by now. You are going through some things because a life-altering event happened to you. Your mental and emotional state is yours, not theirs. Some people may empathize with you, but they truly do not know what you are feeling. Your external appearance may not match your internal feelings. People need to respect your journey, not knowing you are struggling day to day. Talking to someone about your feelings is okay. Grieving is okay. Take your time and as much time as you feel that you need.

I don't feel as if I'm the same person I was when Alonzo was alive. The people around me act as if nothing has changed. My tolerance level is low. I try to maintain a peaceful frame of mind to keep my sanity. I try to avoid and ignore people and situations that may irritate me. I avoid meeting new people who are completely unaware of my loss. One of the reasons I avoid meeting strangers who don't know my situation is that people ask general getting-to-know-you questions. They ask about spouses, kids and employment. I will tell a complete stranger that I have no plans on meeting them again and that I don't have any children. That avoids the awkwardness of their sympathy and additional questions.

My weight has always fluctuated within ten pounds. I just want to be able to fit into my clothes and be comfortable. I have been able to maintain a relatively normal and healthy physical demeanor. I could be healthier by working out and eating better. I want to be happy and if eating something helps me find my happy place, then so be it.

I receive the most comfort when I am cuddling and playing with my granddaughter. She is so freaking smart, fun and adorable. I make sure she is safe, protected, loved and cared for as her dad would have wanted.

My hardest moments are around the fifth of the month. Alonzo's homicide occurred on the fifth, and my mind always seems to know when that day is approaching. Alonzo's birthday on May 28, and death anniversary are tough for me. I am pretty much a nervous wreck during those times of the year. It doesn't help that the dates are relatively close together.

My fear used to be death and the unknown. I now could care less. I don't think that I have any fears. I am not suicidal, but I have made preparations for my death by purchasing a burial plot next to Alonzo. I have considered writing my obituary. I have had open conversations with family about my end-of-life plans, so they don't have to worry about things.

For me, hope means justice, closure, being able to go to court and knowing the details surrounding Alonzo's death. I think I would be able to forgive if I knew the reason and circumstance behind his murder. If Alonzo was hurting someone and they were protecting themselves, I believe I would be able to forgive. But I don't think I will be able to forgive a senseless, unjustified murder. They shot him in his backside, he may not have seen or knew it was coming. That is a cowardly, unforgivable act.

My faith has allowed me to be more aware, listen to my purpose, be obedient and act accordingly. I never quite knew or understood my purpose. Why am I here? What am I supposed to do with my life? To find what I believe is my purpose through such a tragedy is a hard pill to swallow. I have a friend who calls it my ministry. The journey and struggle of being a #MommaOnaMission started out as a hashtag. Momma On a Mission, Inc. became incorporated on September 19, 2014. I never imagined in my wildest dreams of becoming an advocate for the families of homicide victims. The people God has strategically placed in my life at various moments is mindboggling. Knowing that each and every moment has occurred at His will, that my son, my (sacrificial) little lamb, may have died to help define my purpose is even a bigger pill to swallow.

Momma On a Mission, Inc. received our 501(c)(3) status on March 23, 2015, and it would not have existed if Alonzo Thomas IV was alive. I would not be in the community hugging total strangers who have experienced the same devastating loss, speaking publicly, having relationships with funeral homes and knowing about resources pertaining to violent crimes. I am able to speak to a family and empathize with them, lend a guiding hand to a journey I am familiar with. My belief and faith have enabled me to do it.

I have an annual fundraiser on the first Saturday of April called Walk A Mile In My Shoes. It commemorates the anniversary of Alonzo's death, his name, legacy, and raises funds for Momma On a Mission, Inc. It has turned into a day when I recognize other families of homicide victims, provide them with a platform to speak on their journey and raise money for them, as well. Everyone can use some support or a helping hand. I have walked in their shoes and traveled a similar journey, hence the name, Walk A Mile In My Shoes.

When I am asked to tell my story in public, I tell people that Alonzo Thomas IV, my only child is one of Kansas City, Missouri's unsolved homicides. He was murdered by someone he was familiar with. His homicide occurred around people who he associated with.

We are in need of the public to speak up and help to put the pieces of the puzzle together. There is a thirteen-thousand-dollar reward for information leading to an arrest in Alonzo's case. If you have any information that will help get justice for Alonzo, please call the Tips Hotline at 816-474-8477 (TIPS).

MONIQUE WILLIS, Alonzo's mom

MommaOnAMissionInc.org

FROM DENNIS N. GRIFFIN

Thank you

I want to extend my sincere gratitude to the writers and to all who contributed to this book in one way or another, and to those who have supported and encouraged my efforts. You gave your time and energy without financial compensation and no guarantee of results. Without you, this project would probably never have gotten off the ground, and almost certainly would not have finished.

I will be forever appreciative of your selflessness and dedication to a very worthwhile cause.

May God bless you, each and every one.

DENNIS N. GRIFFIN
The Transparency Project

SURVIVORS

Meet the Writers

*

KAREN BEAUDIN

Karen is an author and speaker who addresses the subject of unsolved homicides to institutions including law enforcement, and universities during training seminars, conferences, and criminal justice programs. Past speaking engagements include Suffolk New College in Ipswich UK, Unsolved Homicide Training Course for Ohio's  Bureau of Criminal Investigations, and as keynote speaker at the 10th Annual National Missing Persons Conference.

Media interviews include Elizabeth Vargas on 20/20, Bob Ward with Crime Reporter from Fox News Boston, and Sean MacDonald, Andy Hershberger, and Ray Brewer from WMUR TV. In 2009, Karen and her sisters were influential in establishing New Hampshire's first cold case unit.

During Victims' Rights Week 2010, the Gloddy family received a certificate of appreciation from New Hampshire Governor John Lynch for their outstanding service on behalf of victims of crime. In 2012, the Ohio Attorney General recognized Karen for her advocacy in promoting cold case units. Also, the Fraternal Order of Police in Ohio recognized her for her valuable contribution to Ohio's law enforcement community and the Ohio Unsolved Homicides Initiative.

CONTACT:
ksbeaudin@gmail.com | www.karenbeaudin.com
A Child is Missing: A True Story | A Child is Missing: Searching for Justice
The Kirby Boys Adventure Searching for the Lost Key (Children's Book)
Grief Diaries: Surviving Loss by Homicide | Grief Diaries: Project Cold Case
Survivors – The Forgotten Victims of Murder and Suspicious Death

*

LISA M. BUSKE

Lisa was born in a small town in Oswego County, New York. She and her husband, Ed, are empty nesters of one daughter, Mary. Lisa has enjoyed writing since first grade when her teacher, Mrs. Emerson told her she was a good writer and would be an author one day. Lisa never forgot these words of encouragement despite her father telling her to get a real job to support her writing endeavors. Lisa's positive attitude and sense of humor are genetic and helped her survive after the abduction of her only sister, Heidi M. Allen, on April 3, Easter Sunday, 1994.

Lisa utilized her A.A.S. In Humanities and B.A. in English and Professional Writing as avenues to improve her knowledge of writing before pursuing the publication of her first books, "Where's Heidi? One Sister's Journey" and "When the Waves Subside There is Hope" in 2013. Since then she's published a few more books.

Lisa is a teacher's assistant at the local elementary school, a job she enjoys this so much that going to work isn't work, it's a joy. She looks at her career as an opportunity to invest in the future of the children she works with. Lisa also encourages and inspires others to see the positive side of life through her blog as well as her podcast, Livin' with Lisa: Keeping it Real, available on most podcast apps. Lisa shares life with an honest and fun-loving attitude through both written and spoken words. From tragedy to triumph, Lisa shares the message it is possible to survive, even after tragedy and loss.

She values friends, family, and the kids at school. Lisa recognizes each day is a gift and counts each moment a blessing and opportunity to encourage others. Decades after her sister's loss, the grief brought her to her knees and one student told her what she needed, God. Since then, she tries to set aside her own loss and grief to help others.

CONTACT:
Phone: 315-288-6962 | Email: lbuskewriter@aol.com
Website: www.lisambuske.com | Blog: www.lisambuske.com/blog
Podcast: https://anchor.fm/lisa-buske
Facebook.com/LivinwithLisa | Facebook.com/WheresHeidi
Twitter: @LisaBuske | Instagram: Livin_with_Lisa | Amazon: Lisa M. Buske

*

PHYLLIS ANDERSON COOK

Phyllis was the only girl out of four children born to Dan and Frances Anderson in the small country town of Bonifay, Florida. She and her family later moved to Pensacola, where Phyllis married and had two children. She was always very protective of her three brothers and had a special, nearly psychic, connection to them. She was always able to sense when something was wrong or they were hurt.

On September 25, 1967, Phyllis had a bad feeling that Ronnie, her little brother, was in danger. The very next day, she received word that Ronnie had been shot and was dead. At first, she was told he had died by suicide, but her instinct said that wasn't true. She knew he had been murdered. In the fifty-one years since, Phyllis has never given up in her quest for answers and justice for Ronnie.

On April 18, 2003, her nightmare was relived as her father, Lt. Dan Anderson of the Harrison County Sheriff's Department, was found dead, shot in the head just like Ronnie. His death was also ruled a suicide.

Her love and devotion have kept Phyllis on a long and difficult journey for justice. She vows to never give up until the coldblooded killer or killers of her brother and father are identified and brought to justice.

*

TAMMY DOWNS

Tammy was born and raised in South Carolina. She has two sons and two grandsons. She was thirty-eight years old in 1966, when her sixty-five-year-old father Jack was stabbed to death at the Rosewood Boat Landing in Columbia, South Carolina. Since her father's murder, she has been on an exhaustive campaign to keep her father's story alive and the investigation into his death active. She has vowed not to give up until her dad's killer is identified and brought to justice, no matter how long it takes.

CONTACT:

Facebook.com/coldcase1996unsolved

*

DONNA FEW

Donna Few was a single mother of five children living in the mountains of North Carolina, for much of her adult life. When she turned thirty, she closed her business, Vegetarian Café, and moved the family to Durham. She enrolled in the paralegal program at Durham Community College. While completing that course she worked as a victim's advocate for the Orange-Durham Coalition Against Domestic Violence and also at Rape Crisis of Durham where she served on the state board of directors. In addition, she served as a court advocate and crisis hotline volunteer from 1990 to 1994. She relocated to Brevard, North Carolina, in 1994, and opened Bearfoot Café.

Following the murders of her daughter Mariah and son Hank in 2012, it has been her mission to uncover the truth about her children's deaths. In 2014, she filed a wrongful death suit against ten people she believes were involved in her son's murder. The discovery process has brought new information to light showing a law enforcement cover-up.

In January 2012, Donna founded a nonprofit soup kitchen and opened Cashiers Tailgate Market. Every Thursday, the soup kitchen served over a hundred free meals until 2017, when Donna had to leave her home because of death threats.

*

GERRI HOUDE

Gerri is a registered nurse in Massachusetts. She was seventeen when her sister Theresa was murdered in 1978. After raising two daughters, Gerri decided to embark on a mission to see that the cold case of her sister's death was properly investigated.

To that end, since 2015, she has been actively pursuing cold case legislation to give families access to case files, and has been working to keep Theresa's case in the eyes of the public.

On December 17, 2018, the Massachusetts State Police along with the Norfolk County DA erected a billboard with Theresa's picture and contact information for the public to submit tips. It is with these continued efforts on the part of law enforcement and families that Gerri believes there will be justice for Theresa.

*

TONI INGRAM

Since her daughter's stalking and murder, Toni's family has faced an immense amount of resistance trying to have the case investigated. Her journey has made her realize that her case is not the only case like this. In summer 2012, less than a year after her daughter's murder, Toni became a victim advocate and began working with victims of stalking starting with www.morgansstalking.com. Through her blog, she helps stalking victims from all walks of life,

Toni then became a volunteer for Families of Homicide Victims and Missing Persons (FOHVAMP), a nonprofit organization in Colorado. She served as an advocate for families who had sought help, and eventually became the west coast director for FOHVAMP.

Toni found that working with others in the same situation helped her own heart to heal. Being of service to others has helped her find happiness in her own life and she's grateful that she was given the opportunity to remind other families to never give up.

CONTACT:
www.unresolvedhomicides.org

*

CARLA M. JACKMAN

Carla Jackman grew up in Grafton, Massachusetts. Along with her sister Karen and brother Rick, Carla spent summers at the family cottage on South Pond in Sturbridge. She was thirty with two children, ages five and seven, when her niece Holly was abducted from the family cottage and murdered in 1993.

Carla believes that so many folks think something awful like stranger abduction only happens to others. They like to think they have things all figured out, and don't have to think about the reality that sexual predators exist. That is naïve and potentially dangerous. Carla's family still owns the summer home, but the fun times became so clouded by the horror that they no longer use it—they rent it out.

Carla and her husband divorced shortly after Holly was murdered and she raised her children on her own. She is happily remarried and the proud grandmother of a four-year old. She enjoys her job as a secretary at an elementary school and doesn't miss a chance to remind students to memorize their parents' phone numbers in case they're ever caught in an emergency situation. She is vigilant with school attendance and follows up on every child not reported absent. But mostly, she enjoys seeing the enthusiastic youngsters with so much potential learn and grow.

*

TWYLA JOHNSON

Twyla was born in Des Moines, Iowa. She has three brothers and had one sister, Diane Schofield, who was murdered in 1975. She also has two children and one grandchild. She is a stay-at-home mom who, since her sister's still unsolved murder, has relentlessly pursued finding out who killed Diane and bringing them to justice.

Justice delayed is justice denied, and Diane's murder has been unresolved for far too long.

*
LACEY KEARNS

Lacey Kearns wasn't yet born when her aunt Brenda Lacombe was murdered, yet Lacey is determined to be an advocate for Brenda and her family, and also help other families of homicide victims whose cases remain unsolved.

Lacey first began investigating her aunt's death while doing some family research. She found an old letter Brenda wrote a few months before she died. This brought back memories of when Lacey was a kid going to the library with her mom, who looked through newspaper reels for articles on her sister. Her mom spent a great deal of time searching for answers to Brenda's death, to no avail. At the time, everything her mother tried was a dead end. Lacey empathized with her mom, feeling the defeat she felt.

As Lacey began to fill in the gaps where her mother left off, she started assembling documents and made notes of discussions she had with people who worked on Brenda's case or had knowledge of it. She soon began to see how history can leave a trail, and every contact leaves a trace. Lacey feels fortunate to have met so many incredible people from different backgrounds who teach and support her in all her efforts.

Lacey's dream is to someday live in a world that is encompassed by true liberty and justice.

CONTACT:
avoiceforbrenda@gmail.com
Facebook.com/avoiceforbrenda

*
DIANA MARIA PIERCE

Diana is first a woman of God and a woman of faith. She was born in Canton, Mississippi, and lived in Mobile, Alabama, with her aunt and uncle until she was five. She then returned to Canton and began school. After high school she took college courses in ministry and also enrolled in H&R Block Tax School and has been preparing taxes ever since. In addition, she has been involved in the hospitality industry for over thirty-two years.

Although never married, Diana gave birth to two strong healthy boys, Vito and DeColbie (Coby). Although Coby was murdered when he was intentionally run over by a vehicle in 2012, when asked how many children she has, she always says, "Two." Since Coby's murder, Diana has labored tirelessly as an activist in Chicago. She is currently working with other parents and detectives to get countless other cold cases solved, including Coby's.

Diana enjoys international traveling and always takes with her the shoes Coby was wearing when he died. She wrote a song for Coby called "Peace and Love Coby," and performed it with the Chicago Symphony Orchestra.

*

LISA SANCHEZ-LUCERO

Lisa was born and raised in Albuquerque, New Mexico. She graduated from high school and attended community college. She married her husband in 1978, and had two children. In 2001, Lisa and her husband inherited their two nephews when her sister died. Lisa was a construction office manager  and was in the industry for over thirty-five years. She retired in 2009, to care for her disabled son and elderly mother. She is currently a loving homemaker who devotes her energy into seeking justice for Michael, her nephew who was murdered in 2013.

*

DONNA UNDERWOOD

Donna Underwood was born in Sulphur Springs, Texas, a small town in Hopkins County. She married Danny Underwood and is now the mother of two grown children. Staci, the youngest, lived at home, while Daniel, the oldest, had been living on his own and raising his own family since high school. Donna worked as a bookkeeper, secretary and dispatcher for a local company, retiring after more than twenty years of service. She then did volunteer work through her home church, which required many long hours and became her passion.

The Underwoods were a close-knit family and had contact with Daniel at least two to three times a week. They enjoyed regular family get-togethers, with lots of food and domino or card games. There was never a dull moment as the grandchildren ran about and played. They were living a normal and quiet life, or so it would seem at the time.

Donna's world was turned into a dark tangled web starting with a single phone call she received in the early morning of September 4, 2008. She was told Daniel had been shot and the prognosis was not good. He was pronounced dead within a few hours. Since that day she has been on a long and tortuous search for the truth. Year after year she has been Daniel's voice to the world, as he continues to speak from the grave. Her volunteer work and faith became the foundation that has kept her grounded in the aftermath of losing her son.

*

MONIQUE WILLIS

Monique Willis was born in Los Angeles and raised in Kansas City. She received her high school diploma in 1991, from Southwest Science Math Magnet in Kansas City.

In 1993, her only child, Alonzo Thomas IV was born. She then continued her education and in 1998, received her A.A. from Longview Community College in Lee's Summit, Missouri. In 2006, she obtained her B.A. from DeVry University in Kansas City. In 2011, she welcomed her granddaughter, Zoey, to the world and in 2014, she welcomed her grandson, Alonzo V, into the world (he never had a chance to meet his dad).

In 2014, Monique founded Momma On a Mission, Inc. to serve as an advocate for families of homicide victims, to keep Alonzo's memory alive for the legacy of his children, and to help families who have suffered the traumatic loss of their loved one by helping them through the grieving process while standing by their side to fight for justice.

ABOUT

DENNIS N. GRIFFIN

Dennis Griffin retired in 1994, after a twenty-year career in law enforcement and investigations in New York State. He wrote his first novel, "The Morgue," in 1996. He has since written and published a total of eight mystery/thrillers. In 2001, Dennis turned his attention to nonfiction and began writing "Policing Las Vegas: A History of Law Enforcement in Southern Nevada." He currently has nine nonfiction books in print.

In 2017, Dennis founded the Facebook group The Transparency Project. Mission Statement: The goal of The Transparency Project is to help families who are survivors of victims of murder or suspicious death, to gain access to police records related to the investigation of the death of their loved one. This will primarily involve making sure the police agency involved is complying in full with the Sunshine or Open Records laws in effect in their particular jurisdiction. It can include filing appeals when requests for records are denied and/or recommending changes to existing laws that are overly restrictive.

Dennis is the host of the popular podcasts Crime Wire and The Transparency Project Radio Show. He also serves as a consultant, matching true crime movie and documentary producers, writers, and event coordinators with potential technical consultants and speakers for their projects or events.

CONTACT:
Facebook.com/groups/199487740806089

ALYBLUE MEDIA TITLES

WWW.ALYBLUEMEDIA.COM

A Child is Missing: A True Story
A Child is Missing: Searching for Justice
Grief Diaries: Through the Eyes of a Widow
Grief Diaries: Project Cold Case
Grief Diaries: Surviving Loss by Suicide
Grief Diaries: Victim Impact Statement
Grief Diaries: Surviving Loss by Cancer
Grief Diaries: Surviving Loss of a Spouse
Grief Diaries: Surviving Loss of a Child
Grief Diaries: Surviving Loss of a Sibling
Grief Diaries: Surviving Loss of a Parent
Grief Diaries: Surviving Loss of an Infant
Grief Diaries: Surviving Loss of a Loved One
Grief Diaries: Surviving Loss of Health
Grief Diaries: How to Help the Newly Bereaved
Grief Diaries: Loss by Impaired Driving
Grief Diaries: Loss by Homicide
Grief Diaries: Loss of a Pregnancy
Grief Diaries: Hello from Heaven
Grief Diaries: Grieving for the Living
Grief Diaries: Shattered
Grief Diaries: Poetry & Prose and More
Grief Diaries: Through the Eyes of Men
Grief Diaries: Will We Survive?
Grief Diaries: Hit by Impaired Driver
Grief Diaries: Surviving Loss of a Pet
Real Life Diaries: Living with a Brain Injury
Real Life Diaries: Through the Eyes of DID
Real Life Diaries: Through the Eyes of an Eating Disorder
Real Life Diaries: Living with Endometriosis
Real Life Diaries: Living with Mental Illness
Real Life Diaries: Living with Rheumatic Disease
Real Life Diaries: Through the Eyes of a Funeral Director
Real Life Diaries: Living with Gastroparesis
Color My Soul Whole
My Grief Diary
Grammy Visits From Heaven
Grandpa Visits From Heaven
Faith, Grief & Pass the Chocolate Pudding
Heaven Talks to Children
After-Death Communication: God's Gift of Love
Grief Reiki

Humanity's legacy of stories and storytelling
is the most precious we have.

DORIS LESSING

*

PUBLISHED BY ALYBLUE MEDIA
Sharing stories that need to be told.
www.AlyBlueMedia.com

CPSIA information can be obtained
at www.ICGtesting.com
Printed in the USA
LVHW011730171219
640803LV00004B/680/P

9 781950 712014